Status For Sale
The Complete Guide to Instant Prestige

Status For Sale

The Complete Guide to Instant Prestige

By

Wayne Yeager

Charter Publications

3119 Isabel Drive Los Angeles, CA 90065

Status For Sale
The Complete Guide to Instant Prestige

Copyright © 1992 by Wayne Yeager. All rights reserved. No part of this book, in part or in whole, may be reproduced, transmitted or utilized in any form or by any means, electronic or mechanical, including photocopying, recording, or by any information storage and retrieval system, without permission from the author. Permission is not necessary for quotations in reviews or articles for periodicals, television or radio.

Printed and bound in the United States of America

Current Printing:

10 9 8 7 6 5 4 3 2 1

Publisher's Cataloging in Publication
(Prepared by Quality Books Inc.)

Yeager, Wayne B., 1966-
   Status for sale : the complete guide to instant prestige / Wayne Yeager.
   p. cm.
   ISBN 1-881248-00-3

   1. Social status. 2. Prestige. 3. Social acceptance. I. Title. II. Title: The complete guide to instant prestige.

BF637.S8Y3 1992   647.7
                            QBI92-10465

This book is sold for entertainment and information purposes only. The author, publisher and distributor(s) will not be held accountable for the use or misuse of the information contained herein.

Contents

Foreword by Dr. Jeffrey Lant	9
Introduction	11
Chapter One: Instant Background	**17**
A Picture is Worth a Thousand Bucks	20
Further Suggestions For The Home	20
What's In a Name?	22
Accent-uate The Positive	23
Ah... The Old Country	26
Your Brilliant Military Career	26
College - The Easy Way	28
Honorary Doctorates	31
The Easiest Real Degree	32
Instant Ivy League	32
Instant References	33
Friends For Sale	34
First I'd Like To Thank...	35
Members Only	36
Other Club Tips	39
Heraldry and Genealogy	40
Chapter Two: Prestigious Titles	**43**
Religious Titles	44
Aristocratic Titles	46
Noble Titles	56
Capitalizing on Your New Title	60
The Ultimate: Becoming Royalty	61
Chapter Three: Prestigious Occupations	**65**
Occupations in the Arts	66
Money Occupations	75
Power Occupations	78
Adventure Occupations	83

Chapter Four: Weird Credentials For Sale — 87

Chapter Five: A Day in the Life of a Status Symbol Master — 91

Chapter Six: Prestige Addresses — 99

Chapter Seven: Status While Traveling — 101
Getting There — 101
Once You're There — 103
Hotel and Restaurant Tricks — 104
Great Seats — 106
The Phony Holiday — 107

Chapter Eight: Fame and Immortality — 109
Instant Expert — 109
Getting in Who's Who — 110
Best Dressed Lists — 112
Beauty Contestology — 112
Fame For Sale — 113
Statues and Plaques — 116
Immortality via Contributions — 116
Immortality Unlimited — 117
Your Place in the Cosmos — 118

Chapter Nine: More Status For Sale — 119
Seeing and Being Seen — 119
Spring Training — 119
International Contacts — 121
SuperDad — 122
Backstage Passes — 122

Swiss Bank Accounts	123
Own a Piece of America	123
Royal Warrants of Appointment	123
Boards of Directors	124
"Fantasy Island" by Mail	125
The Ultimate Newsletter	125

A Final Note   127

Foreword

Wayne Yeager is a clever young man who has discerned an essential aspect of our very superficial age: **to seem is to be**. It no longer matters where one has come from... not even what one has accomplished. The **only** thing that matters is what other people think. This is what status is all about... and this is why securing status is more important today than ever before.

The problem is, while having status is more important than ever, knowledge about how to get it is often maddeningly elusive. Generally, the means of securing things that will elevate oneself and one's family in the esteem of others remains a very closely guarded secret shared only among a select group of people who deem themselves worthy of having it. Status, after all, is a process of excluding the vast majority from things they may wish to have, so that they can admire the tiny minority they see enjoying them.

This to Wayne Yeager is an entirely unacceptable state of affairs. Although a child of privilege himself, he has determined that the means of securing status be available and open to anyone intelligent enough to take the necessary action to secure them. This shrewd little book is the result of his determination.

Here you'll find an astonishing array of the good things of the world... things that will improve your life, your self-esteem and, most importantly of all, your standing in the eyes of the only people who matter: all the other people in the world who haven't got a clue how to get these things and will respect you extravagantly (if often enviously) for having them.

For that's just the point: you *can* have them, and Yeager, himself the Baron of Montfort, shows you precisely what you must do to get and enjoy them today. For why wait? The wonderful thing about this book is how easy it is to transform your life... without having to do any of the arduous work of locating and investigating these necessary sources of status. Wayne has done all that for you - and amply so.

But one proviso, please. Read this enjoyable little book, study it closely and by all means use it to enhance your position. However, as you more easily and gracefully ascend the social ladder because of what you've gathered here, kindly do not reveal your sources. You see, having status necessarily precludes telling others how you acquired it. That must forever remain an enigma. Just say you've been helped by your very special friend, the Baron of Montfort and, as for the rest, mum's the word. Now you've truly arrived.

Dr. Jeffrey Lant
Cambridge, MA

Introduction

If money can't buy happiness, it can, I discovered while researching for this book, buy just about everything else: power, excitement, fun, friends, respect, and most importantly in these image-conscious times, status. Our perceived status confers our rank in the hierarchy of success, and although status is rarely an end in itself, it is the basis on which the world decides how it shall treat us. And since most people want to be treated well, the quest for status and prestige is, and has been for quite some time, a global obsession.

Once upon a time, status was conferred upon individuals who truly deserved it. They were honored for the deeds they were known to have performed or something less tangible such as aristocratic birthright. But as the world grows more and more anonymous, much social interaction is taking place between individuals who hardly know each other. Therefore, greater importance is placed on superficial appearances, rather than first-hand knowledge of one's actual position. As a result, the world at large judges us less by our true importance in the grand scheme of things, and more by the status symbols we possess and display. These status symbols, which rarely take physical form these days, suggest to the people we fleetingly encounter in everyday life our wealth, our educational background, our tastes, and to an enormous degree, our self-worth. The value of these status symbols, therefore, cannot be over-estimated.

This book is rather like a catalog, listing companies, organizations, and individuals who offer various modern status symbols which, once purchased, bestow upon the new owner a level of prestige that far outweighs the purchase price. You won't find typical and obvious status symbols, such as the Rolls Royce or Brooks Brothers suit here, but techniques for procuring more subtle and even more respected items, such as coveted invitations, bargain Corcorde tickets, or titles of nobility. A few of the suggestions in this book will seem ostentatious and even vulgar to some readers, but status is a very relative thing. What may be considered desirable and prestigious to one social group may be worthless to another social group and vice-versa.

Topics in this eclectic catalog run the gamut from the whimsically harmless, such as where to buy fake cellular phones, to the quite serious, such as agencies that can, ah... "arrange" diplomatic appointments in Third World countries. Listings toward the more serious end of the scale may not remain at the given address indefinitely. People who sell fake Rolexes and college degrees tend to change addresses now and then. That is why I have given my own address at the end of this book, so that readers can obtain a list of address updates and new discoveries since publication. Eventually, obsolescence is a problem for all books of this variety, but this will be a step in the right direction toward solving this problem.

It is now time to tackle some of the other questions that will inevitably surface due to the controversial nature of this particular subject. If the Old Guard aristocracy is offended by such a notion as outright status purchase, it's time for a brief lesson in the long history of status as a commodity. Prestige has been for sale from the beginning of recorded history - it is just now becoming an exact science.

Take baronets, for example, respected members of the English ruling class, who style themselves Sir and Lady Lastname. Though technically commoners, baronets have entree into the elite social circles of Britain, and the title is just as inheritable as the Crown of England. Pretty prestigious, right? Well, the original baronets became so by donating about 1,600 Pounds Sterling to King James' royal coffers in the early 17th century. The king sent his friend, the Duke of Buckingham, across the countryside, and if you wanted a title, and had the cash, your name was simply filled in on the blank letters patent. *Et voila...* instant aristocracy!

The Roman Catholic Church also knew a hot commodity when they saw one. During the Middle Ages, popes often sold "plenary indulgences" to all comers. These certificates of sin absolution were no doubt handy documents to have while out raping and pillaging. Likewise, our heroic ancestors who held highly-respectable military commissions perhaps did so because their wealthy relatives arranged it with the officers in charge, a not uncommon practice prior to World War I. Few descendants of these aristocrats of gentle birth are aware of these ancient practices, and probably wouldn't admit it if they were. Buying prestige may seem to be an invention of the self-indulgent '80s, but it is actually very deep-rooted in human history.

Although our predecessors may have gone to absurd lengths to gain influence, notoriety, or attractive positions, the antiquity of status-buying may not alleviate the feelings of impropriety or even guilt that you may harbor. Well, while this is a decision which must be made on an individual basis, there is really no need to be embarrassed by such acts. If flashing a Gold Card, riding in a limousine, or owning impressive credentials makes you feel better about yourself, or affords you preferential treatment, or helps you attain your goals, then it is certainly money well spent.

Everybody... EVERYBODY tries very very hard to appear smarter, more important, and just plain better than they really are. Is it any wonder why people buy houses and cars far beyond their means, why garbage men grandiloquently call themselves "sanitation engineers", or why potential employees fudge a bit on their resumes? Not at all! The simple truth is, people insist on displaying a level of affluence that they haven't yet achieved. It's a universal trait. And if this is an accurate description of you, get ready; this book will show you many ways to facilitate the process.

Finally, you may be asking yourself, if people find out that these things can just be purchased outright, where is the prestige? After all, if you could simply buy an Olympic Gold Medal or an Academy Award, there would hardly be any glory in owning one, right? Well, this is a deceptive question, for the answer is contingent upon exactly how many people know that it was, in fact, bought. You see, if no one but you knows that your Ferrari was actually built from a replica kit, or that you paid to have your latest novel published, or that you hired a publicist to get you on "Donahue", the status that these situations confer is still virtually irreproachable. Here's an example:

Before 1939, the tiny country of San Marino would dress its entire army in parade uniforms, march through the streets in your honor, and for a grand finale, have you created a Duke. To the rest of the world, you were a distinguished, if new, nobleman. To the discreet president of San Marino, however, you were just another satisfied customer.

With the astounding variety of self-help success books that abound today, I was somewhat amazed that no one had ever written a step-by-step guide to the purchase of that elusive asset we call status. Even if someone had, it would probably have only scratched the surface, for in this age of instant gratification, status-buying opportunities are constantly being created to keep up with the demand.

I don't make any claims that this is the definitive,

complete directory of modern status symbols, but it is, I feel, a representative sampling of what is currently available. And, after reading this book, I believe you'll agree that happiness is still about the only thing that remains unbuyable. Happy Shopping.

Wayne Yeager
April 1992

Chapter One:
Instant Background

Anyone seeking a shortcut to success should recognize the intrinsic value of status symbols. These symbols, when strategically flaunted, can create fantastic opportunities, impress casual bystanders, and help you win friends and influence people. The largest and consequently most important of these symbols is what we call "background," for without it, all other achievements are somehow cheapened, and become inconsistent and less prestigious. Background is so valuable a status symbol because hardly anyone consciously perceives it as such. It is seen as an unpurchasable asset, something which must be earned or inherited. While this is the traditional way of achieving it, it is sometimes possible to contrive some of its various elements, so that background is instantly manufactured.

Background really is a difficult word to precisely define. Wholly inadequate is my pocket dictionary's definition: "a person or thing's origin." While this is sometimes true, origin is far too vague a term to be helpful here. Background, in this context, tells the world your social class, genetic make-up, tastes, values, education level, and much more. And since everyone has a social class, genetic make-up, tastes, values, etc., everyone has background; it's just that some individuals' background is much more attractive, and thus more conducive to success, than others'. The purpose of this chapter is to offer solutions to those who wish to bring their's up a notch or two.

While it's impossible to change the past, it is possible to scrape together a few things now that you should have been born with (had your parents enough foresight), and to retroactively bestow status upon your earlier days. It is also possible to acquire certain articles that conjure up images of hard work, wealth, and power. And, of course, to be true to this book's title, you will see how to obtain these things the easy way: by buying them. But before we examine specific background buying opportunities, let's look at some general tips to get you started down the road to Statusville.

For example, the best way to move up socially is to move physically, since your hometown or neighborhood will always judge you by your humble beginnings. Even if you become president of your own multi-million dollar corporation, win the Miss America pageant, or save the planet, you will always be known to the local gentry as the upstart son or daughter of that used-car salesman. A number of national celebrities have commented in the past that their own hometown doesn't realize, or care for that matter, just how famous they really are.

Once you've selected a city or neighborhood where the natives are more easily impressed, or where you are completely unknown, you'll need a dwelling that reflects your soon-to-be-elevated position.

The best home bargain for the upwardly mobile is a run-down mansion, the older and bigger, the better. To prevent visions of a paint-covered Tom Hanks in "Money Pit" from keeping you awake nights, take along a home improvement specialist when old house hunting. He should be able to give you a rough estimate of the costs involved to get the house into shape. Actually, these old mansions can often be had cheap, and offer an instant Early American background to the buyers. Modern-style homes are okay, but no matter how luxurious they may be, there will always be that "nouveau" taint to your perceived wealth, which may result in being snubbed by the Club, or a cold reluctance in a handhake from an "upper." An added bonus of the old house trick, especially in a larger town, is after the necessary painting and repairing is done, further status can be garnered by throwing a few, "I cahn't believe the fahmily let it go to such hell, rahly I cahn't"'s arround town.

To reinforce your newfound Early American background, one that will imply a long history of prominence in your family, you'll need to go in heavily for antiques. Not wagon wheels, coffee mills or other flea-market garbage, but heirloom quality furnishings that look as though they've been in the family for decades, if not centuries.

For both economical and utilitarian reasons, you may opt to use antique reproductions in your home furnishing plan. These reproductions are often indistinguishable from the originals in all but the most rigorous examinations, they cost only a fraction of what the originals do, and they can actually be used without fear of damaging irreplaceable family treasures. Some of the better companies selling reproduction pieces through the mail are listed above. You can write for their catalogs, the prices of which follow each address.

Ballard Designs
1670 DeFoor Avenue
Atlanta, GA 30318
catalog: $3

The Bombay Company
P.O. Box 161009
Ft. Worth, TX 76161
catalog: $2

Georgian Gallery, Ltd.
5157 Richland Avenue
Kansas City, KS 66106
catalog: $5

Also in our collection, we must have several ancestral portraits, but not necessarily of our own ancestors. It is more helpful to buy portraits of important-looking individuals, preferably in full regalia or military dress. These are available at just about every upscale antique shop in the country, and they're not very expensive. After all, who wants old portraits of people they don't know? You do.

Think of it as reverse adoption. Now no visitor to your new home will have memorized your complete genealogy, so a well-placed "It's so nice and inspiring to have ancestors hanging about" can do wonders for background seekers. And this is not complete misrepresentation. After all, they are *somebody's* ancestors.

A PICTURE IS WORTH A THOUSAND BUCKS

While we're on the subject of portraits, I wanted to remind you that you may consider having one of your own painted. Almost no one outside the upper-middle class sits for a real oil-portrait anymore, so this simple act is really quite a bargain from a status standpoint. However, for an even greater bargain, consider using the services of a mail order artist, such as A.J. Boone, Jr. These artists will paint your likeness on canvas by referring to the photographs you supply them. Will the finished product be as high-quality as the portrait you would get after four or five live sittings? No, but you might want to take A.J. Boone's $34.95 pricetag into consideration. The average price for an oil portrait in my small survey was around $2,000. And if you want to stay trendy, you can't forget Muffy. A number of portrait artists are specializing in favorite pets, and the same mail order bargains are available by sending photos of your favorite furry friends. Mill House Studios is one such company, so write them for prices and details.

> **A.J. Boone Studios**
> 32-36 102nd Street
> Flushing, NY 11369
>
> **Mill House Studio**
> P.O. Box 448
> Compton, RI 02837

FURTHER SUGGESTIONS FOR THE HOME

The first status signal a guest encounters when visiting your home is the set of entry gates and driveway. The upper-class rule of thumb on entry gates is - if you can see the house from the road, no entry gates (unless the house is enormous), if you cannot see the house from the road, use them. The driveway rule of thumb is a little more complicated. The general theory here is the longer the drive, the higher the class, keeping in mind that long and curved outranks long and straight. The reason for this, as Veblen noted in *Theory of the Leisure Class*, is the "canon of futility" which demands that the high-status drive be "a circuitous drive laid across level land." Only in this way can you demonstrate your total disregard for practicality. The surface of the driveway is equally important. Asphalt is too utilitarian (and thus contravenes the canon of futility) to merit any serious consideration. The most impressive drives are made of tiny gravel, in a neutral or dark shade preferably, since they must be maintained at great expense and inconvenience.

Next, our visitor's eye turns to our lawn. If our front yard has become a showplace for objects to be admired, everyone knows we are sinking into the depths of blue-collardom. Examples of these lawn *objets d'art* are wrought iron "trees" with each branch holding a flower pot, green shiny spheres perched atop concrete pedestals, truck tires serving as makeshift flower pots, and absolutely anything plastic. The only objects found on the upper-class lawn will be planters, statuary (preferably sculpted), and flowers. But not just flowers, high-status plants like rhododendrons, tiger lillies, amaryllis, columbine, clematis, and, occasionally, roses. Lower down the scale you'll find the more common and brightly colored phlox, zinnias, gladioli, tulips, and petunias.

Once inside the house, the guest will probably be conducted to the living room, the room where the owners attempt to put their best foot forward. High-status living rooms will have at least a ten-foot ceiling with moldings on baseboards, door frames, or on the ceiling itself. There must be a hardwood floor, but mostly covered with old Orientals. There should be at least one bookshelf, but two or three is better, and they should be filled with old leather-bound editions (which are now sold by the yard in used book stores) or newer non-bestsellers.

Since the living room is usually the owners' mini-museum of class symbols, more accurate views of *actual* status are to be had in the bathrooms and kitchen, so you'll want to take special precautions here. The upper-class kitchen is designed to be used only by servants, so it is immediately identifiable by its lack of modern conveniences. There will probably be no dishwasher, garbage disposal, toaster oven and certainly no Formica. The high-tech kitchen enters as you slide down the class scale a bit, where a member of the family has to actually prepare the meals themselves, and as Paul Fussell said in *Class*, the more your kitchen resembles a lab, the worse for you socially. The same goes for bathrooms. The high-status bathroom will resemble the high-status kitchen in its depravity of modern improvements. Scented toilet paper, pink johnny-rugs and blue commode water all testify to the proletariat taste for the "finer things."

Outside again, our guest may visit our patio or deck, a very eloquent class identifier. It should be much larger than necessary, and the furniture should be very comfortable and, of course, organic. Wooden furniture with deep cushions is the classiest, while aluminum chairs with vinyl-strip backs are the lowest. It's an upper-class convention to never be in the slightest way uncomfortable, and if you wouldn't sit on flourescent green plastic indoors, why do it outdoors?

WHAT'S IN A NAME?

More than you probably think. One's name conveys a great deal about its owner, and many aspirants change their birth name to something that more accurately reflects who they wish to be. Under Common Law, this is perfectly legal, and can be done with ease in all 50 states.

A name change can have a drastic effect on how the name-changer is perceived. For example, the perfectly respectably named designer Henri Mathieu is now known as Yves St. Laurent, a name, I suppose, that implies inherent good taste and a hint of Old World aristocracy. And several people have questioned whether movie stars, like Tony Curtis or Kirk Douglas, for example, would have ever achieved their degree of success had they retained their birth names. (Bernard Schwartz and Issur Demsky, respectively.) But entertainers and designers are not the only people who can benefit from name surgery. Anyone may round out their desired image by adopting such names as Rockefeller, Windsor, Rothschild, or anything else that delivers the proper effect.

If this is an avenue you'd like to explore, GRF Press offers a book called *Changing Your Name For Fun and Profit*, which lists, state by state, exact procedures for a legal name change. It also has a few reproducible legal forms you may need in the process. The book is $10 postpaid.

> **GRF Press**
> **2050 Idle Hr. Center**
> **Suite 108**
> **Lexington, KY 40502**

ACCENT-UATE THE POSITIVE

Class distinctions based on accent are not quite as severe in the United States as in England, but such distinctions do, nevertheless, exist. The Bostonians who "pak their caz at Havad Yad," the New Yorkers who see a "boid in a boich tree on Toidy-Toid Street," and the Southerners who manage to utter about one sentence per minute, all suffer a loss of status when dealing with people outside their own geographical region.

In *Live For Success*, John T. Molloy decided to test the socioeconomic signals given off by accents. He gave identicle recorded statements to hundreds of men and women throughout the country, and asked them to identify the economic and educational level of the speaker. A distinct pattern emerged. Strong and easily identifiable regional speech patterns tested for the most part as lower-middle class in regions other than the speakers'. Being a down-home Southerner is okay, as long as one remains in the South, but the accent will convey a lower-class image in just about every other area of the country. The same goes for Brooklynites. Ironically, the best place for an American to be born, according to *Live For Success*, is London. Molloy tested a London cabbie with no high-school education whatsoever, and everyone who heard his recorded statement assumed he was a professional man, and a very competent one at that.

Accents are not the only characteristics of our speech that belie affected status. Lower socioeconomic-level speakers tend to shorten words and chop phrases. Individuals with a blue-collar background are much more likely to say "comin an' goin'" than "coming and going," and will usually shorten "the" to "de", "yes" to "yeah", "no" to "nah", and "isn't" to "ain't." Although these shortened words are heard everyday and can be found in modern dictionaries, they have no place in the vocabulary of the status-seeker.

The way we speak is not entirely our fault. Accents are a product of environment, and our speech patterns usually resemble those of our parents' or others we spend alot of time with. This crippling heritage can be overcome, however, by hiring a personal speech therapist, who can usually help you erase accents and improve any other vocal liabilities you may have. These therapists can be found in the Yellow Pages of any medium-sized city, or you can call the most famous of all, Robert Easton, the Henry Higgins of Hollywood (213) 463-4811. The cost for this personal therapy can be a bit prohibitive, so you may choose to spring for one of the professionally prepared home-study courses now available. A very good program to help cultivate positive speech patterns, and to eliminate that stifling accent is the "Live For Success Speech Course" developed by Dr. William Formaad. Dr. Formaad is the Professor and Director of Communication Sciences and Disorders at Seton Hall University and a Fellow of the American Speech and Hearing Association. This excellent course is on audiocassettes, so you can listen to it over and over again. The cost of the program is $80 postpaid.

> John T. Molloy
> P.O. Box 526
> Washington Bridge Station
> New York, NY 10033

But even though the accent is now eradicated, to be truly accepted into the club, your conversation should be sprinkled with typical upper-class phraseology. Entire books have been written about this subject, but the only thing to remember is that great store is placed in understatement among the uppers. To them, the vulgarity of vulgarities is to actually *try* to impress others, so you must be careful to downplay your possessions. Ideally, such understatement should just come naturally once you understand the basic precept. A very good manual on what to say and when to say it is *Class* by Paul Fussell. It is published by Dorset Press of New York, and can be obtained through inter-library loan.

Instead of	Say
tux or tuxedo	dinner jacket
limo or limousine	car
chauffer	driver
crystal	glasses
china	plates
cocktails	drinks
fresh flowers	flowers
affair	party
home	house
designer towels	towels
imported wine	wine
billiard parlor	pool room
big-screen tv	tv
Cadillac, Mercedes, etc.	car
Ivy League College	school
original oil painting	painting
limited edition lithograph	picture
Louis XV chair	chair

AH... THE OLD COUNTRY

To coincide with your future worldly image, you may wish to adopt a country other than the United States as your "original" homeland. There's no need to forego patriotism; it's simply a business decision. Ordinarily, becoming a citizen of another country requires reams of paperwork, mountains of red tape, and can be an exercise in patience. Actually, the mechanics of expatriating are not all that complicated, but the process is kept shrouded in a misty gloom to discourage would-be Monagasques.

Dr. W.G. Hill, an international consultant and lawyer, has prepared an interesting book called *The Passport Report*, which shows how to literally *buy* citizenship to many countries while retaining full U.S. citizenship privileges. In most cases, the process can be completely executed without leaving the country. In addition to status enhancement, dual nationality offers some excellent tax benefits as well. *The Passport Report* is available directly from the author, and costs about $100 plus postage.

> **Scope Books, Ltd.**
> 62 Murray Road
> Horndean, Hants
> PO8 9JL,   U.K.

YOUR BRILLIANT MILITARY CAREER

Even if you were never actually in the armed forces, you can enjoy the instant background derived from becoming a *faux* veteran. All you need is a rank and the usual military paraphernalia. Both are pretty easy to buy.

American Guerilla Force, a national paramilitary group, sells commissioned officer ranks to all comers, and at the time of publication, you could get the rank of Lieutenant for $15, Captain for $25, and for Colonel,

> **AGF**
> P.O. Box 4972
> Falls Church, VA
> 22044-4972

expect to pay about $50.

Likewise, Prince de Galbo de Polignac, self-proclaimed descendant of the Kings of Bohemia, will award you the rank of Captain in his "Legion of Honor" for a donation of seventy-five dollars. As the Prince says, it's a "fraternity of men who are brave in defending right, whose honor is untarnished, and whose loyalty to principle and family is undoubted." And, presumably, who are willing to cough up the seventy-five bucks.

> **Prince de Galbo**
> **C.P. 875**
> **Succursdale**
> **Dejardins**
> **Montreal, Quebec**
> **H5B 1B9 Canada**

Not all military-style ranks that are available cost money. The Salvation Army, for example, bestows ranks all the way up to General, and the Honorable Order of Kentucky Colonels, like a few other Southern charitable institutions, can make you a real, honest-to-goodness Colonel for simply filling out a few forms. You don't have to be a resident of the state that confers the Colonelcy, and you are entitled to use the rank in all matters, both personal and business. And, unlike Colonel Sanders, you are not required to wear a white suit and string tie. These groups, which survive solely on member contributions, expect you to make a small donation every year, but it certainly is not mandatory.

> **Honorable Order of**
> **Kentucky Colonels**
> **P.O. Box 20702**
> **Louisville, KY 40220**

After you have your desired rank, you'll probably want to show off your military exploits. For Congressional Medals of Honor, Purple Hearts, and other decorations and ribbons, Quincy Sales and Sidney B. Vernon can supply all your needs. And to announce affiliation with your favorite branch of the service, you'll want to buy Army, Navy, Air Force and Marine uniforms, warm-ups, shirts, ties, rings and dog-tags from U.S. Cavalry, a gigantic mail-order outlet at Fort Knox. This is probably the world's largest assortment of non-surplus military gear, and I'm told more servicemen patronize them than civilians do. Their current catalog is $4 and is updated three or four times per year.

> **Quincy Sales**
> P.O. Box 700113
> Tulsa, OK 74170
>
> **Sydney B. Vernon**
> P.O. Box 1560
> Wildomar, CA 92395
>
> **U.S. Cavalry**
> 2855 Centennial Avenue
> Radcliff, KY 40160-9000

COLLEGE - THE EASY WAY

Education is obviously an integral part of one's background. However, long ago people realized that education is an awfully hard thing to demonstrate to total strangers, so the diploma was invented to prove that the bearer had undergone some degree of formal education. The idea that it takes a sheet of phony parchment to prove one is educated is rather outdated, but the tradition has been with us for centuries and doesn't seem to be waning in popularity.

Almost as long as there have been real degrees, enterprising crooks have been offering fake ones, and the artificial degree business is now a multi-million dollar a year worldwide industry. The recent government crackdown on these diploma mills, called "DipScam", put enough pressure on the industry to force many mills to close shop, but some have managed to find legal loopholes or evade the Feds long enough to prosper still.

Palmer Enterprises, for example, sells degrees from two non-existent colleges, Franklin University and Bradford University, for about $100 each. For a mere $30 extra,

> **Palmer Enterprises**
> P.O. Box 6606
> Altadena, CA 91001
>
> **University Novelty**
> P.O. Box 5172
> Tampa, FL 33675
>
> **National Certificate Co.**
> 210 Fifth Avenue
> New York, NY 10010

you graduate Summa Cum Laude! University Novelty offers thirty different degrees from the college of your choice for about $250, plus they will provide transcripts for an additional $90. National Certificate sells Bachelor and Master degrees "novelties" from eight invented schools, such as Adams Institute of Technology and Eastern University. National Certificate has escaped legal hassles by requiring all customers to sign a pledge that these novelties are to be used as "wall decorations only." Their prices are typically around $60 for each degree.

For those who wish to have a fake degree from a real university, Edgar H. Hurlock has designed an ingenious do-it-yourself kit. For $50, you get a very impressive-looking pre-printed parchment certificate and a sheet of Old English transfer letters. Using these letters, you can print the college name, your name, type of degree, and graduation date, and the end-product looks remarkably authentic.

> **Edgar H. Hurlock**
> 71 Dalewood Avenue
> Fairfield, CT 06430

The prestige of a British degree can be had by writing the Sussex College of Technology. One can purchase just about any degree (except law and medicine), and have their choice of three different certificate styles. For an extra $170, you will be made a Fellow of the college, with the supreme privilege of adding the FCST suffix to your name. I was told that they also sell transcripts as well, and will even backdate degrees up to 30 years, but you will have to write them for current information and prices.

Thanks to the separation of church and state, most religious bodies are allowed to confer non-academic religious degrees, such as Bachelor of Theology or Doctor of Divinity. Universal Life Church is perhaps the most famous (infamous?) DD bestower in the country, but so many people know about ULC, it's probably a good idea to go elsewhere for your doctorate. For example, Charter Ecumenical Ministries will confer upon you a Doctorate of Divinity for only $20, and you get a beautiful degree-size certificate and the right to call yourself "Doctor." Is all this legal? Yep.

> Sussex College of Tech.
> Dept. NAA/1
> "Highfield"
> Dane Hill
> Haywards Heath
> Sussex RH17 7EX
> England
>
> Universal Life Church
> 152 Thompson Avenue
> Mtn. View, CA 94043
>
> Charter Ecum. Ministries
> 3119 Isabel Drive
> Los Angeles, CA 90065

Universal Life Church sued the Federal Government for the right to do so, and it is this trial that serves as the landmark case for religious degree issuance. The court, in deciding for ULC, said:

> "The court must address itself to the defendant's (the Federal Government's) second conclusion: that the ordination of ministers, the granting of church charters and issuance of honorary doctor of divinity certificates by the plaintiff are substantial activities that further no religious purpose. Certainly the ordination of ministers and chartering of churches are accepted activities of religious organizations. The fact that the plaintiff distributed honorary doctor of divinity certificates is of no moment. Such activities may be analogized to mass conversions at a typical revival or religious crusade...
>
> "Neither this court nor any branch of government will consider the merits or fallacies of a religion. Nor will the

court compare beliefs, dogmas and practices of a newly organized religion with those of an older, more established religion. Nor will the court praise or condemn a religion, however excellent or fanatical or preposterous it may seem. Were the court to do so, it would impinge upon the guarantees of the First Amendment."

Amen.

HONORARY DOCTORATES

The advantage of the honorary degree is the fact that you can *buy* a doctorate from a highly respected, accredited university for a few thousand dollars. Granted, the degree is honorary, and thus non-academic, but the owner is given the legal right to use "Doctor" before his or her name, so this is really quite a value.

Basically, there are two ways to obtain an honorary doctorate. First, you can actively solicit the degree directly from the university in which you are interested. One Los Angeles businessman even ran ads in various magazines offering to donate $10,000 in return for an honorary degree from any accredited college. When Dr. John Bear, author of *Bear's Guide to Non-Traditional College Degrees*, contacted him he told Dr. Bear that he had in fact received the degree, but graciously declined to say from whom.

The other way to obtain an honorary degree is to watch for advertisements placed by the universities themselves. Several colleges with urgent financial needs, and some with not-so-urgent financial needs have placed national ads lately suggesting that donations (which, incidentally, would be tax-deductible) would be rewarded by conferring honorary doctorates or even board positions upon the donors. In 1982, an advertisement appeared in the *Wall Street Journal* offering a trusteeship in the highly-respected Embry-Riddle University for a $1,000,000 tax-de-

deductible contribution. As universities find this to be a viable source of quick income, more and more honoraries will be offered for sale in the near future. Keep your eyes open and check the intellectual and business magazines, as it seems these tend to attract the biggest share of this type of advertisement.

THE EASIEST *REAL* DEGREE

The easiest accredited degree in the world is the Bachelor of Arts degree from Thomas A. Edison State College in Trenton, New Jersey. Edison will allow you college credit for life experience, taking tests, and even watching videotapes. The whole process can be completed in a year, at home, at a cost of about $3,000.

> T.A. Edison State College
> Admissions Office
> 101 W. State St., CN 545
> Trenton, NJ 08625

Thomas A. Edison State College is accredited by the Middle States Association of Colleges and Schools, and its graduates have attended over 150 graduate schools, including most of the Ivy League. All things considered, this is the quickest, easiest, and cheapest respectable degree in America.

INSTANT IVY LEAGUE

Everybody knows that Ivy League schools are hard to get into, expensive to attend, and pretty challenging so lots of status and instant background are bestowed upon the students at these institutions. Few people know, however, that many of these schools have adult, summer, or extension programs that are both inexpensive and relatively easy, yet allow the student to experience nearly the same level of prestige as the regular undergraduate. In fact, for the trifling sum of $1,000, you can have the lifelong privilege of saying you attended Harvard or Oxford, which for background alone is quite a coup.

Below are some of the addresses of the mentioned programs, and if you're interested, write for details.

> Harvard Extension School
> 20 Garden Street
> Cambridge, MA 02138
>
> Cornell's Adult University
> 626 Thurston Avenue
> Ithaca, NY 14850
>
> Oxford/Cambridge Univ. Vacations
> International Building
> 9602 NW 13th Street
> Miami, FL 33172
>
> Yale Summer and Special Programs
> 53 Wall Street
> New Haven, CT 06520
>
> Vassar College
> P.O. Box 300
> Poughkeepsie, NY 12601
>
> St. Aldates College-Oxford
> Rose Place, St. Aldates
> Oxford OX1 1SB
> ENGLAND

INSTANT REFERENCES

Anyone needing good, quick job references, or simply wishing to create a job history can make their own by buying the "W-2 Kit" from Antidote Press. Along with

> Antidote Press
> 1442 E. Lincoln
> Suite 173
> Orange, CA 92665

blank W-2 forms, blank corporate letterheads and other goodies, a guidebook explaining how to pull this off is included. The book also tells you how to get sterling references from your Congressman. I don't imagine that all of the stunts in this book are completely legal, so please use your discretion. This interesting kit costs about $20.

FRIENDS FOR SALE

Like most people, you probably already have a close circle of friends with which you play golf, go shopping, or whatever, but how can butchers and secretaries and janitors offer instant background? Sadly, they cannot. It's been said that we are the average of our combined acquaintances, so in order to boost your average, you'll want to cultivate a secondary, well-connected circle of friends for just that purpose. And since most of these new "friends" you'll be buying are status-seekers themselves, you can ride their social coattails to greatness.

The trick is quite simple. If you have the means, temporarily retain some of the most well known, socially prominent professionals in your area. A month or two shouldn't cost that much, and this should be plenty of time to launch your friendship campaign. Go after the most prominent doctors, attorneys, therapists, accountants, decorators, real estate agents, consultants, artists, plastic surgeons, or anyone else you find worthwhile.

After you've become a client, casually suggest tennis or dinner or whatever seems appropriate. If you've followed some of the suggestions in this book, you should by this point be totally acceptable as a social companion. Once this social meeting commences, the target "friend" should be absolutely inundated with the similarities, coincidences, and preferences that the two of you share (you did do your homework didn't you?), and made to feel that fate herself has mandated your friendship. After all this, the target should feel guilty if he or she chooses not to invite you to the next social event. And, in this economy, they will probably do anything necessary to keep you as a client.

FIRST I'D LIKE TO THANK

For all those glorious achievements in your life that went unrecognized, now you can award yourself. Trophyland USA sells hundreds, no... make that thousands of trophies, ribbons, certificates, medals, plaques, and awards for just about any occasion imaginable. Just browsing through their catalog is guaranteed to make you feel like a miserable, underachieving failure. They sell to anyone and their prices are reasonable. Write for their free catalog.

> **Trophyland USA**
> **7001 W. 20th Avenue**
> **Hialeah, FL 33014**

Nice award certificates are available from Dinn Brothers and can be made to be any award the purchaser so desires. At ten cents apiece, you can cover an entire wall with your many admirable deeds. A more varied selection of certificates can be had from Bale Company, a major high-school and college supplier. For a mere two dollars, you can be a Valedictorian, Salutitorian, or member of the National Honor Society, with a lovely cord and tassel presentation folder to house each prestigious document. You can also buy the highly-coveted "Bus Driver Safe Driving Award" if you promise not to let it go to your head.

> **Dinn Brothers**
> **68 Winter Street**
> **Holyoke, MA 01041**
>
> **Bale Company**
> **222 Public Street**
> **Providence, RI 02940**

MEMBERS ONLY

According to *The Right People* by Stephen Birmingham, once upon a time, a prominent Philadelphia family was reading the obituary of their newly deceased patriarch. "Mr. Prominent," the newspaper said, "was a member of the Philadelphia Club and the Racquet Club." The family was mortified. The deceased man's son called the editor and demanded a retraction. "He was a member of the *Rabbit* Club, not the Racquet Club," the son announced. The editor apologized and said, "But does it really make that much difference?" The son exploded, "It makes a *world* of difference, a *world!*"

The Victorian sentiment that you can judge a man by his club is probably as true today as ever, and for those seeking instant background, joining the right clubs is a must. You must eschew such plebian groups as the City Bowling League or any group whose name has the words "Ancient" or "Elks" in it.

Essentially, there are three tiers to the club pyramid, with each tier representing an increased level of "entry difficulty." Sports clubs have the lowest "E.D." since all that is required is money. Genealogical and historical societies have a medium E.D. level, since many require proof of blood descent from certain people, or are limited to certain numbers, or are by invitation only. And, of course, the highest are the private clubs, which require you to know one or more current members and be personally recommended by them.

You will probably want to join a sports club or two, and the sports you select must reek of wealth and/or good taste. The racquet sports - tennis and squash - have long been almost mandatory upper-class pastimes. Squash and tennis, according to Birmingham, are suffused with an aura of easygoing good-fellowship, and have a breezy, casual air about them that blends well with the society manner. Golf, once the mainstay of the *haute monde*, has suffered a social reversal, and has become a little too egalitarian for ardent status-seekers. If you have enough savvy to gain admittance to a private country club, that's okay, but typically, private tennis or squash clubs carry more clout.

Further up the prestige ladder you have the horse sports, such as thoroughbred racing, fox hunting and, of course, polo. All that is required for entry into these clubs is a knowledge of the sports and the means to participate in them. Sometimes the proper equipment can set you back several thousand dollars, but still, it's nothing more than a money game. At the top of the sports club ladder is the elusive yacht club. These, too, require a substantial outlay of cash, but frankly, little else. To discover your nearest polo or yacht club, you can write their respective national headquarters.

> **U.S. Polo Association**
> **4059 Iron Works Pk.**
> **Lexington, KY 40511**
>
> **Yachting Club of USA**
> **P.O. Box 487**
> **Islamorada, FL 33036**

Since appropriate attire is a necessity in these sports, below are some companies that offer polo and fox-hunting uniforms, and yachting apparel and supplies.

> **Wind in The Rigging**   **E & B Discount Marine**
> **125 E. Main Street**   **201 Meadow Road**
> **Port Wash., WI 53074**   **Edison, NJ 08818**
>
> **Rick's Saddle Shop**   **Kauffman's**
> **P.O. Box 96**   **419 Park Avenue**
> **Englishtown, NJ 07726**   **New York, NY 10016**

It is also a good idea to join a historical or genealogical society or two to display the high regard you have for your illustrious ancestors. On page 38 is a list of the most prestigious such clubs in the United States. Joining any of these, plus your local or state historical society should be all that is required in this department.

The Augustan Society
P.O. Box P
Torrance, CA 90507

Polish Nobility Assn.
529 Dunkirk Road
Anneslie, MD 21212

Assn. of German Nobility
1638 S. Norton Avenue
Los Angeles, CA 90019

First Families of GA
15 Watson Drive
Newnan, GA 30263

First Families of VA
c/o Mrs. C.M. Seaman
5055 Seminary Rd. #439
Alexandria, VA 22311

Daughters of the
   American Revolution
1776 D Street, NW
Wash., DC 20006

Baronial Order of
   Magna Carta
c/o Frank Robinson King
20 W. Front Street
Media, PA 19063

Descendants of Signers of the Dec. of Ind.
c/o G.M. Bielenstein
560 Riverside Drive
New York, NY 10027

General Society of Mayflower Descendants
P.O. Box 3297
Plymouth, MA 02361

Order of the Descendants of Colonial Governors
2546 Cedar Avenue
Minneapolis, MN 55404

Russian Nobility Association of America
971 First Ave.
New York, NY 10022

OTHER CLUB TIPS

Although you may know you're a genius, you can prove it to the world by joining Mensa, the international high-IQ society. Their policy is to accept for membership only those applicants who score in the top 2% on standard IQ tests (currently about 132) or achieve a predetermined score on one of their other qualifying exams, such as the ACT, SAT or GRE. One can simply take and re-take the various tests until the necessary score is achieved. Once you've arrived at geniusdom, a certificate proclaiming your brilliance and other Mensa paraphernalia is available. Write them for a brochure and the name of the testing proctor in your area.

> **American Mensa, Ltd.**
> **2626 E. 14th Street**
> **Brooklyn, NY 11285**

If you want to enhance your resume or simply impress your mail carrier, you can join the International Society of Millionaires. Judging from their literature, they are not all that particular about whom they let join, and you will certainly not have to submit a financial statement.

> **Internat'l Society of Millionaires**
> **117 W. Harrison Building #I-148**
> **Chicago, IL 60605**

You can also be a member of a prestigious club without the hassle of actually joining. Huh? That's right - simply buy the club tie and you're pretty much in. Club ties are the badges that tell those in the know that you served with a particular regiment or attended a certain school. Wearing a tie with a design representing a club or organization with which you are not affiliated is almost considered a felony in England, and simply isn't done. In fact, most British clothiers require club identification before selling certain ties.

Land's End, however, has a large selection of college, club and regimental ties, and do not care if you belong to the organization or not. If Land's End does not have the particular tie you are looking for, another good source is Humphreys of Kent, England. They will make a tie to your exact specifications, and are quite reasonable. Write them first for complete information.

> Land's End
> 11 Land's End Lane
> Dodgeville, WI 53595
>
> Humphrey's
> Sandtiles House
> Sandling Road
> Saltwood, Hythe
> Kent CT21 4QN
> England

HERALDRY AND GENEALOGY

Coming from a well-to-do family is a crucial aspect of background, and in some higher social circles, it's a must. Fortunately, you can easily fend off questions about your family's prominence by simply indicating their obsession for privacy. But it might be a good idea to have some tangible evidence, such as a coat-of-arms and a few well-known ancestors to toss about during conversation.

After your historical investigation to uncover prominent individuals with the same surname, the Royal Colleges of Spain and England will make you an armiger by drawing up and recording an original coat-of-arms in your name. It is a fallacy held by many people that a coat-of-arms belongs to an entire family and therefore can be used by anyone in that family. While coats-of-arms are indeed inheritable, they are bestowed upon individuals, not families, so to think that one can claim a crest that once belonged to anyone with the same surname is ridiculous.

Once the *letters patent* are received, gentlemen officially acquire the title of Mister, although most men have taken the liberty of using that title all along. To request a grant of arms, write to either College of Arms listed below, and expect to pay about $1,000 for their services. Once you receive your grant, you will officially appear on the records of the Royal College as being an armiger, that is, "a person granted and having the sole right to the particular arms designated to him."

One trick that is useful for status-seekers is the oldest-living-ancestor gambit. Instead of seeking a grant of arms for yourself, or, arranging to have a title (as we'll see in the next chapter) bestowed upon you, you should try to get this honor for your father or grandfather, so that you, in effect, inherit *their* armourial bearings. This lifts the onus from your shoulders of seeming to be a self-promoter, and lends instant antiquity to your family's coat-of-arms, thereby increasing your status.

> **Duque de Campobello**
> **Inst. Heraldica de Espana**
> **English Speaking Offices**
> **National House, Santon**
> **Isle of Man (U.K.)**
>
> **Royal College of Arms**
> **Queen Victoria Street**
> **London, England**

Once you get your official crest, you can really flaunt it by purchasing a ring with your coat-of-arms engraved on it. Heraldica Imports takes some liberties with the historical traditions of heraldry, and if your surname is not on their list of armigerous surnames, why, they'll just invent a crest for you free of charge. Their gold rings cost between $300 and $1,000, and you can even get the image reversed to make wax-seal impressions for that important correspondence.

> **Heraldica Imports**
> **211 W. 46th Street**
> **Room 1004**
> **New York, NY 10036**

Finally, if you want to go completely overboard with this heraldry business, you can buy a custom-made heraldic flag from Fly Your Colors, a company run by one of the country's top vexillologists. The flags cost about $50 each and are just the thing to hang from your box seat at the opera or carry during your next crusade.

Fly Your Colors
607 Ruby Street
Redondo Beach, CA
90277

Chapter Two: Prestigious Titles

Titles are perhaps the oldest status symbols in the world, and even today are among the most prestigious. Titles evoke an air of ancient power and wealth, and people who possess the right ones are virtually guaranteed entry into the *haute monde*. The mystique of these ancient honors makes many people feel that a title-holder is inherently special, and thus deserving of red-carpet treatment. In fact, most individuals who would not so much as speak to you will gladly bow and curtsy when they discover you are a bishop or a duke.

Before you discover how to make your way to this illustrious position, it's time for a crash course in titular semantics. As a general rule, titles are bestowed upon an individual by a higher authority, whether that higher authority is simply your boss or a representative of God Himself, and range in importance from the extremely common variety, such as Mr. and Mrs., to the royal titles, like King, Queen and Emperor. Between these two extremes, there are religious titles, such as Reverend, Saint, or Pope; the aristocratic titles, such as Knight and Lord of the Manor; and finally the noble titles, like Baron, Count or Duke.

Obviously anyone can use the common titles, such as Mister, so there is no prestige at all in them. Of course, one *could* bestow one of the higher titles upon oneself (much like Napoleon did when he crowned himself Emperor), but anyone pretending to a title lacks the ability to back up the claim, leaving themselves open to being exposed as a fraud. There are a number of watchdog genealogical groups around the world, and being listed in one of these purists' ominous publications such as the *Dictionary of the False Nobility* will wreak havoc on the career of even the most cunning social climber. In fact, there may even be legal reasons to jump through the proper hoops, since people have been arrested for illegal use of noble titles in Germany, where the right to use "Von" in front of your surname is taken very seriously.

The most common way (and some may say the only proper way) to obtain a real title is by actually earning it. This can mean anything from being elected to it, inheriting it, saving another's life for it, or causing miracles to occur for it. Well, "earn" is an awfully subjective verb, so I would suggest anyone in the market for a title "earn" it as easily as possible. There are many competent title-granting authorities who will gladly bestow one honor or another upon you for the right "donation." A quick perusal of history shows that obtaining honors through outright purchase or by way of donations in one form or another has been a fixture since time immemorial.

If you are using titles as a vehicle to status, keep in mind that this is a three stage process, and that the procurement of a title does not mean your work is complete. No, no, no. You must plan your transubstantiation - the debut of the newly-titled you. You've got to decide just how you are going to present your title to the world, and finally, how you are going to capitalize on it. There are some loose guidelines to follow, but this is a highly individualized process, so you'll have to decide for yourself just how to proceed.

RELIGIOUS TITLES

Charter Ecumenical Ministries has made Reverends out of thousands of ordinary people, and will do the same for you if you send them $10. This is undoubtedly the best title

> **Charter Ecumenical Ministries**
> 3119 Isabel Drive
> Los Angeles, CA 90065

buy in America today, for with these credentials, you can declare your home a church (with the accompanying tax advantages), perform marriages and funerals, and enjoy airline and hotel "clergy" discounts.

For a donation of $50, you can move up the religious scale a bit, and have Calvary Church of Faith bestow upon you the title of Bishop, with the right to be addressed as "Your Grace." There is no work to do, no real responsibilities, and you don't even have to be a Christian to qualify.

> Calvary Church of Faith
> P.O. Box 333
> Rillton, PA 15678

For the full effect, you may wish to order one of the various religious uniforms from Almay and Sons. They have all the surplices, cassocks, and frocks (and all those other bits of clothing you've never known the names of) that a man of the cloth could ask for.

> Almay and Sons
> 37 Purchase St.
> Rye, NY 10580

Traditionally, to be canonized - that is, officially recognized as a Saint - you have to be dead. For many people, this strict policy detracts somewhat from the appeal of sainthood, but that's just the beginning. A department within the church hierarchy (in the Vatican, it's called the Sacred Congregation of Rites) has to proclaim that not only were you blessed, which incidentally is hard to prove, but that you were also responsible for two miracles during your lifetime or after death. So with these stringent regulations, no wonder some Saint-wanna-be's have sought help elsewhere. Yes, if the title of Reverend or

> Universal Life Church
> 152 Thompson Ave.
> Mtn. View, CA 94043

Bishop is a little too bland for an individual of your distinction, you can, for only $10, become an official saint of the Universal Life Church. And to prove it to those skeptical friends of yours, they will send you a beautiful parchment certificate with your saintly name engraved on it.

Just as it's difficult to become a saint of the Catholic Church, becoming a Pope is no mean feat, either. You have to first become a priest and work your way up the ranks of bishops, archbishops and cardinals to become a member of the Sacred College. Next, you have to wait for the current Pope to die. At this point, the members of the College go into conclave, shut off from the outside world, to choose a new one. This is where your years of campaigning finally pay off. If a conclusive vote is reached in your favor, it will be signaled to the eager world by puffs of white smoke.

But doesn't that seem like an awful lot of work for a fancy title? It sure does! That's why the Church of the Sub-Genius will be happy to make you a Pope for just $10 or so. Needless to say, the Church of the Sub-Genius has quite a few Popes. In case you're wondering exactly what you're becoming Pope of, the Church is open to those with IQs up to 139.5, and believes that the saviour, one J.R. "Bob" Dobbs, the living slack master, will save the doomed planet at 7:00 AM, July 5th, 1998 by helping all Sub-Genii flee to safety. Farfetched? Maybe, but you never can be too sure. Write the "church" for details.

```
Church of the Sub-Genius
P.O. Box 140306
Dallas, TX 75214
```

ARISTOCRATIC TITLES

What once was a reward for bravery and superior fighting skills has become something of an elite club.

Knighthoods are conferred today for civil and military achievements as well as excellence in the arts, culture and the sciences. Usually a prospective knight has performed some outstanding service in one of these fields, and the sovereign decides to extend their "grace and favour" by dubbing them into their order of chivalry. Sometimes, however, this "outstanding service" can be as simple as donating the right amount of money to the right people.

Although Queen Elizabeth won't sell them, there are ways in which a British knighthood may be *bought*. Her Majesty bestows knighthoods upon individuals from all over the British Commonwealth, from such locales as Pitcairn Island and Tuvalu. Now obviously, the total lack of competition means a wonderful deed performed at one of these obscure locations will carry much more weight toward a knighthood than the same deed performed in the middle of London.

One gentleman of the author's acquaintance traveled often to one such island on business, and soon became friends with all the key government officials - all SIX of them. After learning that a schoolhouse needed to be built, and the cost would take a substantial chunk of the government's budget, the businessman volunteered to underwrite its cost. Our shrewd and crafty hero made it politely known that what he wanted in exchange was a knighthood. Not surprisingly, he received just that due to the recommendation of the entire island government.

Getting a knighthood in this manner is a very costly affair and one had better be prepared to spend several thousand dollars. But for those who demand a British knighthood, this is definitely the most direct route. The first step is to become acquainted with the people in power. This includes not only the government officials, but also the clergy, doctors and attorneys. Second, find something that the people need or want badly, but that the government itself can't or won't purchase. Third, offer to supply the thing out of the goodness of your heart, while letting it be known that gosh... if they *insist* on rewarding your gift to humanity, well, a knighthood sure would be nice.

While we often think of Britain when we hear of Sir So-and-So, England certainly has no monopoly on knighthoods. In fact, the combined orders of chivalry in the United Kingdom make up only a small fraction of the total number of such orders around the world, so let's take a look at some of the ones we may be able to join.

The Knights of Malta

Perhaps the most famous and illustrious of all orders of knighthood is the Order of the Hospital of St. John of Jerusalem, variously called also the Sovereign Military and Hospitaller Order of St. John, Knights Hospitaller, and most commonly, the Knights of Malta. The order was begun when one Gerard de Martignes organized the "Friars of the Hospital of St. John of Jerusalem" to aid Christians who had fallen ill during their pilgrimage to the Holy City.

Between 1113, when Pope Paschal II officially recognized the order, until the early 16th century, the Knights Hospitaller moved headquarters from Jerusalem to Margat to Acre to Cyprus, and finally to the isle of Rhodes. In Rhodes, the order got stronger and their priories, or franchises, in Europe went on to amass great wealth. They were involved in numerous campaigns and they eventually, with the help of the king of Cyprus, even captured Alexandria.

One of the most colorful and heroic stands in the annals of medieval military history took place as one of the grand masters, Cardinal Pierre d'Aubusson, successfully defended the island of Rhodes against the assault of the Turkish sultan, Mohammed II. Finally, however, the knights were forced to capitulate to the Turks, thus losing Rhodes forever. At this point, the order fell into disarray and was not fully organized again until the Holy Roman Emperor, Charles V, gave them the island of Malta in 1530.

The Maltese langue of the knights, headed by the Marquis de Vella Haber, is still headquartered in Malta itself. There are, however, quite a number of early branches, each with its own fully-recognized grand master, and each with its own entry requirements. Although members pay dues of about $500 annually, membership in these orders cannot be purchased outright. The Knights are a close-knit brotherhood and one must be nominated by three existing members, then approved by the grand master. I did, however, find one ecumenical langue of this order that is not quite so strict.

HRH Prince Alexis d'Anjou de Borbon-Conde-Dolgoruky, who is a cousin of King Juan Carlos of Spain, heads the Spanish chapter of the Military and Hospitaller Order of St. John of Jerusalem, Ecumenical, of Rhodes and Malta. This langue seems to be much more helpful than the others, and will even connect you with the appropriate sponsors. The donation required for investiture is approximately $2,500, and the yearly membership dues are about $550.

> **Grand Priory UK**
> **Knights of Malta**
> **Hospitallers House**
> **London WC1N 3XX**
> **England**

The Roman Catholic branch of the order, the *Ordine Sovrano di Malta*, is a bit different and more complex. One must be Catholic, of course, and must first receive a recommendation from one's archbishop. Although no donation is required up front, passage fees that may add up to as much as $10,000 are required

> **Ordine Sovrano di Malta**
> **4/6 Cavalieri di Malta**
> **Roma, Italy**

upon approval for membership. And since there are also some hereditary requirements, this one is a tough nut to crack. However, this branch has legal sovereignty as a nation and can even print its own postage stamps.

The Imperial Order of Charles V

This order is not nearly as old as the Knights of Malta, but it is quickly gaining a reputation for its illustrious roster. It is also one of the few such orders which can be arranged completely by donations, and is made all the more prestigious when one considers that its grand master is a member of the Spanish royal family.

HRH Prince Don Enrique de Borbon y de Borbon dubs new knights each year at the Alcazar de Segovia, the famous medieval castle outside Madrid. I was knighted into the order in 1990, and it was a very impressive affair. Full of pomp and ceremony, the investiture is a scene right out of history, with royalty, nobility, movie stars, and miscellaneous VIPs looking on. If you have a reasonable history of civic and social achievement, the Overseas Herald of the Spanish College of Arms should have no trouble getting you in.

> **Overseas Herald
> College of Arms
> National House-M
> Santon, Isle of Man
> British Isles, UK**

The Imperial Institute of Chivalry

L'Institut Imperiale de la Chevalerie, a non-profit organization devoted to the furtherance of chivalric traditions, has some pretty impressive connections, and can arrange your entry into many of Europe's prestigious orders of chivalry for the proper donation. You can write them for their book, *Honor and Glory: Joining the Historic Orders of Chivalry*, which shows how they can help you join these and other illustrious groups:

The German Order of the Griffin

This order was founded in the 18th Century and was a state order of the Grandy Duchy of Mecklenburg-Schwerin. The monarchy of Mecklenburg came to an end in 1918 upon the conclusion of the First World War. The order was revived in the 1980s as a charitable order of knighthood and now is handed out each year in Mannheim, Germany. It is recognized by the Haute Academie de la Chevalerie located in Geneva, the supreme accreditor of chivalrous orders. Total cost for joining is about $1,500.

The Scottish Order of Saint Andrew

This venerable Scottish order has its titular seat at Camster Castle in County Caithness, Scotland. The order has many historical associations including the Royal Stuart Society of Great Britain, and enjoys wide prestige. Joining is a matter of having a sufficiently impressive *curriculum vitae*, and a pledge for a donation in the $2,000 to $5,000 range.

The Order of the Cordon Bleu du Saint Esprit

This is a newer order yet one of the most prestigious. It is Germanic and members include: Otto von Hapsburg, Dutch ex-Premier Dries van Agt, Henry Kissinger, Prince Consort Hendrik of Denmark, German Foreign Minister Hans Dietricht Gensher, and a host of top ranking NATO generals and European politicians, as well as performers like soprano Anneliesse Rothenberger, baritone Marco Bakker, and senuous Dutch filmstar Willeke van Amelrooy. They give tremendous bashes every few months, and the last one my friend attended was heavily covered by the European media. Initial cost for membership is about $1,800 and dues are approximately $420 annually.

Before sending any donations for knighthoods, you'll need to read their book, *Honor and Glory*. It gives the who, what and where of the orders mentioned above, as well as a few others. The book costs $15 and is available in English.

> **Institut Imperial de la Chevalerie**
> P.O. Box 1721
> Hamilton HMGX
> Bermuda

Other Orders of Chivalry

Once In A Lifetime can also arrange some very interesting and prestigious orders. For example, the *Orla Dialago Polskie*, or Poland's Order of the White Eagle, which was founded in the 1500's by King Jan Sobiesky, has been awarded to Kings, Queens, military leaders, and other VIPs for centuries. The last direct descendant of King Jan has revived the order, and all new recipients receive the accolade at a nice induction ceremony in a Polish cathedral. These titles are officially recognized by the government of Poland and are very, very highly regarded. Until the order is completely on its feet, a good friend of the grand master is allowing Once In A Lifetime to offer membership into the order on a limited basis.

Also available is the Military and Hospitaller Order of St. Lazarus, thought to be one of the oldest orders of chivalry in the world. Although some historians date it as early as 125 BC, the order adopted its present form in the mid-11th century and since then has been inextricably linked to all matters of European chivalry. In fact, I believe that this is the highest one can go with respect to knighthoods, and is certainly the most prestigious order one can join for a price. The grand master of the order is the Duke of Seville, a member of the Spanish royal family. Once In A Lifetime can arrange many more orders of knighthood, so

> **Once In A Lifetime**
> 9205 SE Clackamas Rd.
> Suite #419
> Clackamas, OR 97015

send $5 and an SASE for their comprehensive brochure of all their services.

One of the most inexpensive knighthoods I could find is available from Nobilitat Regalia for about $300. Prince Douglas de Clermont is the grand master of the Order of the Commonwealth and the Order of St. Andrew of Jerusalem. These orders are unique, interesting, and apparently quite legitimate, and enjoy a roster of several distinguished members including Peter Cushing, Vincent Price, the Crown Prince of Portugal, and others. The order of St. Andrew of Jerusalem was originally founded in the Holy Land in 1232, and was revived this century. The condecorations of the order are very nice and include moire sashes of honor, as well as neck medallions for formal occasions. Nobilitat Regalia are the agents for the above orders, so you should write to them before sending any money.

> Nobilitat Regalia
> 316 Edward Street
> Victoria, B.C.
> Canada V9A 3E6

For the true bargain hunter, the best low-end knighthood is from the Baronial Order of Saint Lawrence. This politico-religious organization is structured as an order of chivalry, and all members knighted into the order receive the official privilege of adding the "Sir" prefix to their names (or Dame, for ladies). Medallions are also given to be worn on formal occasions or at official functions. For a beautiful parchment certificate, invitations to all annual functions, medallions, and the right to use the knightly title of "Sir" or "Dame," $100 ain't bad.

> Order of St. Lawrence
> 8177 S Harvard #202
> Tulsa, OK 74137

Lords, Lairds and Feudal Barons

Exactly what a feudal barony is in the British Isles is a matter that is subject to much discussion, especially among the English, Scottish and Irish lawyers, since there are slight variations in each region, and no two of them can ever agree on even the simplest definition. However, if we don't bother with the technical details, and look at them merely as an avenue to prestige, we'll find them much easier to grasp.

The feudal barony is a unit of property, the ownership of which entitles the owner to a rank of honor. These ranks do not confer nobility, per se, but are a direct path to elite social circles. In Scotland, the title "Laird" is often used to designate the rank quite similar to that of the feudal baron, while in the Channel Islands, the equivalent rank is called a *seigneury*, and finally, in England and Wales, the rank becomes Lord of the Manor. These titles are tradable commodities and would-be buyers cherish the belief that these titles will "open the castle door to a Camelot of merry peasants, acres of high-society, and retinues of bowing servants," as *World Press Review* puts it. That's not exactly true.

These titles are old - many date back to William the Conqueror - but few of them carry any of the truly useful ancient powers. About all that survives today of these powers, once granted as the pivot of feudal government, is the right of the title holders to call themselves Lord or Lady of XYZ, plus a handful of other small privileges. Apart from the right to shoot game on common land, a feudal baron can gather firewood, cut peat, fish the streams, extract minerals, and in certain situations, charge tolls from passing motorists. One right he can no longer claim is the *droit du seigneur*, which allowed the feudal lord to help himself to village maidens on their wedding night.

In 1906 the Manorial Society was created to keep many of the old documents associated with these lordships, and to protect the interests of Lords of the Manor and Irish feudal barons. Now, most all manor lords belong to this society, which, incidentally, has royal patronage. The

Prestigious Titles

Manorial Society of Great Britain researches and auctions these lordships surrendered by those who need the cash more than the titles, and can cost anywhere from $10,000 on up. The Canadian who anonymously paid $188,000 to become the feudal Baron of Ruchlaw in 1990 set off a mini-gold rush. Scottish and Irish feudal baronies which had been trading at $30,000 suddenly jumped to double that sum. If things continue as they have, these titles may be one of the best investments a status-seeker can make. In 1981, they were going for about $5,000. In 1988, the Irish feudal barony of Kells sold for $40,000. Two years ago, the Barony of Fore and the Channel Island Seigneury of d'Anneville went on the auction block and realized about $60,000 each. Each year the prices get higher and higher and it is rumored that the late Malcolm Forbes, who certainly knew where money was to be made, bought himself such a barony.

For those interested in Scottish feudal baronies, the very best researchers and auctioneers are:

Once a Scottish feudal baron, you'll probably want to become a member of the Convention of the Baronage of Scotland, which maintains a roll of members and is analagous to the Manorial Society in England. The cost of membership is a nominal five pounds per year.

Mrs. David Reid, Sec.
Convention of the
Baronage of Scotland
Robertland, Stewarton
Ayrshire KA3 5JP
Scotland, UK

Aitken and Nairn
Solicitors and Notaries
7 Abercromby Place
Edinburgh EH3 6LA
Scotland, UK

Historic Records Agency
172 Bishopgate
London EC2M 4QN
England

Bernard Thorpe
19-24 St. George
London W1A 2AR
England

With regard to Irish feudal baronies, Manorial Research, the commercial wing of the Manorial Society, often offers these as well as Lordships of the Manor. Strutt and Parker also auctions Lordships of the Manor, and on occasion, Channel Island Seigneuries.

> **Manorial Research**
> 104 Kensington Road
> London SE11 6RE, UK
>
> **Strutt and Parker**
> Covall Hall, Chelmsford
> Essex CM1 2QF, UK

The title of Laird, the Scottish equivalent of Lord, is available at a much reduced rate. The legal department of Queensgate Associates has devised a scheme to provide these Lairdships, along with a coat-of-arms, and legal recognition of the title all for about $2,700. If you're looking for something a little less official, the Great Souvenir Land Company will make you a Laird for about $50 or so. They've purchased a large plot of land in Scotland and have sub-divided it into one square foot parcels. Therefore, when you get the deed to your tiny little farm, you can claim the title of "Laird." The deed is a very lovely document and worth the money whether you want to be a Laird or not.

> **Queensgate Associates**
> Department L
> National House, Santon
> Isle of Man (UK)
>
> **Great Souvenir Land**
> 6 Marine Terrace Mews
> Brighton, Sussex
> England BN2 1AR

NOBLE TITLES

All noble titles today are essentially degrees of honor, and with very few exceptions, they no longer have anything to do with land tenure or official duties. Only in England is the nobility given any legal responsibility, and it could be argued that the House of Lords is little more than an impotent anachronism. Nor do these titles have any money (called entailment) attached to them. Thus stories of unclaimed estates that carry not only titles but fabulous wealth, or that anyone who purchases Arundel Castle becomes the Duke of Norfolk, are pure romantic fiction.

Since Americans usually aren't very fluent in the mechanics of nobility, here are some basic guidelines that may help you in your search for a coronet.

At the bottom of the prestige scale is the baron. This title was originally given to the lords who held small fiefdoms, or land grants, and recognized a sovereign above them. As the title of baron, and most titles for that matter, were associated with the ownership or trusteeship of land, they are often appended with an appellation derived from those lands. For example, one hears of a man being called the Baron *of* Someplace and not Baron Johnson. The wife of a baron, or a woman who is a baron in her own right, is called a baroness.

The viscount, or vice-count, was the medieval equivalent of sheriff. And as the office of sheriff became hereditary, its possessor acquired this title by carring out legal duties and serving the count. The count in turn served the sovereign in his or her palace or royal court. The British equivalent of a count is an earl, the German is *graf*, the French is *comte*, and the Spanish is *conde*. The wife of a viscount is a viscountess, and the wife of a count or an earl, or a woman who is a count in her own right, is called a countess.

If you were charged with the difficult task of maintaining a fiefdom that lie on the border of your sovereign's territory, you were given a special title. The title of marquis, or marquess in England, was bestowed upon those who held and defended such lands. Apparently the name for this title was derived from the medieval word for this border region: *marches*. The title of margrave, the

German equivalent, also stems from this ancient word for the territory they held. The wife of a marquis or marquess is called a marquise and marchioness, respectively.

Finally, we come to the highest non-royal title that a king or queen can bestow: the title of duke. Originally, this was reserved for relatives and at one time was actually higher in rank than prince, but it slowly evolved into a title offered to those performing outstanding service to the Crown, such as the Dukes of Wellington and Marlborough. Of course, the wife of a duke is a duchess.

The above titles are all hereditary, but usually only by the "eldest male legally begotten." If a title-holder has no male heirs, the title can, depending upon local peerage law, pass through the female line, so that a male grandchild inherits the title, or through a co-lateral line, such as the title-holder's younger brother's family. At any rate, no two people can hold the same title simultaneously.

What happens when a title-holder dies with no apparent heirs at all? The title then becomes abeyant, or dormant, until a worthy relative comes along later to exercise his or her claim. Usually after two or three generations pass, a family that may have a right to a title forgets about it completely, and this is where you come in.

A very popular method of obtaining a noble title is by "rehabilitation." That is, rehabilitating, or reviving a title that once belonged to an ancestor, but is now dormant since someone along the line forgot or decided not to claim it. Currently there are hundreds, if not thousands, of extinct titles across Europe (and Asia Minor thanks to the Crusades) that may be properly claimed with the right documentation and a little determination. Surprisingly, almost everyone has such an unclaimed title in their family tree if they dig deep enough. The legal procedure for reclaiming such titles varies wildly, but typically one must prove first that the title is vacant, and second, that they legitimately descend from the last title-holder.

If you supply them with a copy of your known genealogical chart, and the surname you want searched, the genealogical wing of the Ecumenical Orthodox Jacobite Patriarchate of Antioch, one of the prime churches during the Crusades, will search all available historical archives at their disposal to find if any vacant titles exist in your ancestry. The research fee is $280 per surname searched, and you'll probably want to have your mother's and grandmothers' maiden surnames searched as well. You get an individualized report on any claimable titles and full particulars on how to go about getting them. Not only does the Patriarchate search for ancient titles in its own Christian Levant, but it also searches for claimable honors from the historical monarchies of Russia, France, Poland, Hungary, Albania, Portugal, and Naples.

> **Holy See of Antioch**
> **545 Eighth Avenue**
> **Suite 401**
> **New York, NY 10018**

I was able to rehabilitate my barony by using this system, and by virtue of being descended from the last Baron of Montfort, a title that had been absent from my family for over 300 years. The wonderful thing about rehabilitation is the fact that you're getting a title that actually did belong to an ancestor once, so there is not the stigma of actually *buying* a title. However, if the *quid pro quo* method of obtaining honors is something you think you can handle, there are a couple of options open to you.

Since the Vatican demonstrated little or no interest in adjudicating Holy Roman Empire titles after the fall of the house of Hapsburg, the Latin Empire of Constantinople set up a council at Westphalia to preside over these matters. The main purpose of the council is to govern the rehabilitation and issuance of these ancient titles by those demonstrating entitlement, but they also provide a very handy service for status-seekers.

Upon request, the Council of Westphalia will search their archives for an extinct title, one that is unlikely to ever be claimed, and bestow it upon you for a tax-deductible donation to their archaelogical fund or other pet project. These titles are well-researched and documented, and are quite legitimate. First, write the council through the Roman Forum, and ask them to list the extinct baronies, counties, etc. that are currently available.

> **The Roman Forum-W
> 13 Oakleigh Road
> Stratford-upon-Avon
> Warwickshire
> England CV37 0DW**

Be sure to ask for the donation required to receive each, and you'd better send along a couple of dollars to make sure they respond. At press time, the total cost for obtaining a title in this manner was about $1,600, which is totally tax-deductible, making this about the best noble title bargain going.

The Marquis of Alessio is Privy Council for Honors to a number of royal princes, from the houses of Bourbon, Braganza, Lusignan, Paleologus, Lascaris-Comnenus, Anjou, Trebizond, and others, and can usually arrange noble titles and other honors from these individuals in exchange for donations or other good works for favorite charities. The contributions vary substantially from one royal house to the next, so write the marquis for further information. Be sure to include a few dollars for return postage.

> **Marquis d'Alessio
> c/o Postbus 55360
> 3008 EJ Rotterdam
> Holland**

CAPITALIZING ON YOUR NEW TITLE

Whatever your reasons for acquiring a title, you will no doubt wish to enjoy and exploit your new rank to the fullest. Consequently, you must decide on a plan of action to alert your friends, business partners, and colleagues of your new position. Your transubstantiation into your newly titled persona should be done in such a way that you end up being truly honored and not rebuffed and ridiculed for assuming airs.

You must develop a clear image of what the new you will be like, including mannerisms, attitudes, and so on, and develop a plan to gradually bring this image to full flower. I spoke to a number of newly decorated persons to see how they made their social debuts after receiving various titles. The most repeated bottom line, one that seems to be a common denominator in making such debuts successful, is: Be Modest About It (or at least appear to be). Titles are much more effective when *others* talk about them than when you do. Let it be others who elevate you to your proper rank, and never demand such ridiculous things as being addressed a certain way, and if possible, try to look embarrassed by "all the fuss."

The key is to make it clear in advance of meeting someone exactly who you are in rank and importance. If this is done through a third party or otherwise indirectly, people will be predisposed to genuinely honor you. This can be done by having a "secretary" call in your reservations, or organizers of a social function you plan to attend with a question, while casually dropping in your title. There are also those in social groups who tend to be the gossip, and who are genuinely impressed by titles. These people are indispensable, so try and maneuver this type into your presence when your title is announced. The gossip is very useful since through him or her, you have an indirect means of advising all your friends. Tell the gossip about your title "in strictest confidence" to ensure that all your mutual acquaintances will hear about it ASAP.

BECOMING ROYALTY

Perhaps the jewel in the crown of honors, if you'll

pardon the expression, is to go beyond religious, aristocratic and noble titles, and reach the station of royalty. It is the stuff of fairy tales and romantic fantasy. It is also very much an attainable goal for the clever aspirant.

Titles of royalty often confer the right to the qualification of highness, serene highness, royal highness, imperial highness, or any combination of these. The royal titles which may be procured (without actually conquering a nation and declaring yourself King or Queen) are Prince, Princess, and sometime Archduke. Although royalty for the most part is a closed and exclusive club, there are a couple of non-traditional and ingenious ways of joining. In fact, for the right price, almost anyone can become a "royal higness."

All family members of the European royalty usually have minor royal titles bestowed upon them. In other words, the spouse, children and siblings of a sovereign are considered royal as well. And by local law and custom, anyone who is adopted by or marries into a royal family instantly becomes royalty. This technicality is the loophole through which those seeking royal status achieve this feat. This is becoming so common in Germany that its own book of nobility, *Genealogisches Adelsbuch*, refuses to list adopted successors to titles, since the editors call this "cheating."

"Now," you say, "all I have to do is find a royal family member who is willing to adopt or marry me!" Relax - there are several firms that act as marriage and adoption brokers for the status-seeking rich. One is run by Christoph Paikert, a young ex-stock broker who found trading in titles to be more profitable than trading in shares. An arrangement, via Mr. Paikert, for becoming a German count will cost about $70,000, while becoming a Prince or Princess

Christoph Paikert
#1, Ave. Victor Hugo
34200 Sete, FRANCE

with the prefix of HRH, will go for $1,000,000 and up, depending on who is doing the marrying or adopting. Paikert requires a detailed *curriculum vitae* as well as a financial statement from the people he tries to match with nobles and royals. He says he tries to match people who may grow to be good friends so that this becomes more than just a business matter. Or he may just wish to stay within the law; it is illegal in Germany to marry or adopt for financial reasons.

Three more firms that are in the same business as Mr. Paikert are listed here. Kunne was offering marriage and ad-option by Prince Metternich von Hohenzollern for about 1,000,000 Deutschemarks, and Wobst has a large inventory of titles available, from Baron to Prinz. Queensgate has a more detailed price schedule, and seems to be a little less expensive than the others. Send a few dollars when writing to these companies, since they get more than their share of curiosity seekers.

H.J. Kunne
Hainersweg 48
D-6000 Frankfurt
Germany

Frank Wobst
Mittelweg 13
3340 Wolfenbuttel
Germany

Queensgate Assoc.
National House- M
Santon, Isle of Man
UK

Queensgate Associates' 1992 Price Schedule	
Adoptions resulting in a dukedom	$50,000+
Adoptions resulting in a marquisette	$30,000+
Adoptions resulting in lesser title	$20,000+
Adoption into major royal family resulting in royal title	$100,000+
Marriage to duke or duchess	$200,000+
Marriage to lesser nobles	$100,000+
Marriage into major royal family resulting in royal title	$300,000+

Each firm will ask that you send:

1. A *curriculum vitae*, along with some information about your family's background,
2. A financial statement,
3. Two verifiable and preferably prestigious references,
4. Some photographs of yourself,
5. Information about previous marriages, children, and any other personal data you care to share, and most importantly,
6. Information on what you are looking for in the man or woman you seek either to marry or be adopted by, as well as age preference, title preference, etc.

In this sort of adoption or marriage, you will usually be asked to cover the legal and travel expenses incurred in such an arrangement. Usually a pre-nuptial or pre-adoption agreement will be executed by both parties to renounce any claim on the other's assets.

With this particular road to status, one is purchasing not merely the title and royal rank, but rather the whole lifestyle. One is "plugging in", as it were, to the established aristocracy and royalty - not only acquiring a title, but also the connections, the introductions, and the access to the power circles that only royalty provides. For the person of means, this is the most effective method of obtaining the very highest status available.

Chapter Three: Prestigious Occupations

The exact element that determines whether or not a given profession confers status is difficult to pinpoint. Some obvious guesses would be salary or independence, but neither of these really hit the mark. CPAs and plumbers often enjoy tremendous incomes, but precious little status. Nor does the elite occupation require that an individual be his own boss. Attorneys and diplomats hold very enviable positions is modern society, even though one may have senior partners and the other government officials to whom they must answer.

Although we cannot nail it down to a specific feature, we can say that prestigious occupations are those that somehow fulfill the fantasies of those who aren't so fortunate. These jobs conjure glamorous images of money, power, intrigue, excitement, and adventure all rolled into one. In short, everything that the average job *doesn't* offer.

The only problem with these prestigious occupations is their scarcity. One rarely sees "Bank President Needed - No Experience Required" in the help wanted section of the classifieds, and even so, you'd be competing with thousands of applicants. Most of these applicants would be seeking this position for the salary, but you on the other hand, would be seeking this position for its status-enhancing qualities. It is this strategy which will allow you to grab hold of these seemingly better jobs, without the headache of leaving the one that actually pays you. In fact, regardless of your real job, you can create instant status elevation by adopting one of these all-title-no-work vocations.

Until you decide which is the most appropriate for your

particular situation, you should master the fine art of job description embellishment. The trick here is to change the everyday name of your job by describing your duties in a grandiose yet succinct fashion. For example, let's say you pump gas at the corner garage. "Gas station attendant" is not exactly an impressive title, so let's analyze what you do: you transport petroleum from one container to another in exchange for money. You sound like a "petroleum broker" to me. Get the idea?

Instead of being:	Become a:
a caddy	sports administrator
a secretary	executive assistant to...
a waiter/waitress	food distributor
a janitor	internal revitalization consultant
a lifeguard	hydrophobia therapist
a maid	pollutant analyst
a prostitute	recreation advisor
unemployed	non-profit coordinator

When you tire of throwing these trumped-up phrases around when asked what you do, it's time to move on. Here's how to buy your way into something a little better.

OCCUPATIONS IN THE ARTS

Author

There is a very romantic image in the author tirelessly pecking away at the typewriter, churning out the Great American Novel. Notice I said author, not writer. Anyone can *write*; every family has its poor Aunt Gertrude who has written hundreds of short stories which get systematically rejected by every editor who reads them. "Author" is the title given to writers in that elite club reserved for those who've had their work published. The Catch-22 of the writing profession is you can't sell your work unless you've been published, and you can't get published unless you've previously sold your work. But fear not; there are many ways the clever status-seeker can get that novel into print.

When movie stars write their kiss-and-tell autobiographies, or when politicians publish their memoirs, do you think they actually sit down and write it all themselves? Of course not. Most of them simply jot down a few ideas, scribble a couple of anecdotes, and send it off to a "ghost." A ghost-writer is a behind-the-scenes author who writes or re-writes the story, polishes the grammar and sentence structure, and delivers a coherent, publishable manuscript. When an editor gets his hands on this submission, he will probably recognize it as the work of a professional, and will be much more likely to publish it. Ghost-writers work on an hourly, per page or per book basis, and do not require that you give them any credit for their work at all. A dozen or so ghosts advertise in *Writer's Digest*, which is sold on newsstands everywhere.

If, after passing this manuscript around, a major publishing house still won't touch the book, you may want to try a subsidy publisher. These companies will publish your book, no questions asked, but expect you to cover your share of the expenses. Having done that, you will then receive royalties on each copy sold, just as you would from a traditional publisher. This industry has received a bad rap in the past, with these companies being labeled "vanity presses," but every author must start somewhere, and chances are none of the people you are trying to impress will ever know you paid to have it published. If they do somehow find out, kindly remind them that some of the greatest writers in history, including Rudyard Kipling, Ernest Hemingway and George Bernard Shaw, subsidized their work early in their careers.

There are a good number of subsidy publishers that advertise nationally, but if you want as few people as possible to know your intentions, contact an obscure but reputable subsidy publisher such as Phil Dewar Publishing in San Diego. They'll take a look at your manuscript and if they think they can sell at least 1,000 copies, they'll contract with you. After it is published, they will promote, market and distribute the book, and you will receive 50% of all net proceeds. Write them and send $3 for their informative book, *Getting Your Book Idea Into Print*.

> **Phil Dewar Publishing**
> 3808 Rosecrans St.
> Suite 730
> San Diego, CA 92110

Added prestige (and secrecy) can be yours by retaining a foreign subsidy publisher, such as Excalibur Press of England. They do not advertise in the United States so few people will ever know they are not a traditional publishing house. Other foreign subsidy publishers can be found in London's *Sunday Times* and the *International Herald Tribune*.

> **Excalibur Press**
> 13 Knightsbridge Green
> London SW1X 7QL
> England

If you'd rather not hand over control of your book to someone else, consider self-publishing. Not only do you eliminate the stigma of subsidy publishing, but many writers, and very successful ones at that, have learned that they can realize much more profit by supervising the printing, binding and promotion of their book themselves. Any large printer can take care of the actual printing for you, but there are two books you are definitely going to need. First is Jeffrey Lant's *How To Make A Whole Lot More Than A Million Dollars Writing, Commissioning, Publishing And Selling How-To Infor-*

> **JLA Associates**
> 50 Follen Street
> Suite 507
> Cambridge, MA 02138

mation. Lant is often given to bestowing extraordinarily long titles to his creations, but his books definitely live up to their promise. The current price for "Million" is $35 plus postage. The other book you'll need is *The Self-Publisher's Directory*. This book lists most of the major independent book publishers, binders, typesetters, and cover designers in the US and Canada, and also shows you how to apply for and receive an ISBN number for your book as well as a Library of Congress Card Catalog Number. The best part is, it's only $5.95 postpaid.

> Self-Pub'er Directory
> 9205 SE Clackamas Rd
> Suite 419
> Clackamas, OR 97015

Now that your masterpiece is finally seeing print, you may want to access the added prestige of being on a bestseller's list. There are several such lists in the United States, but undoubtedly the most influential is the one compiled by the *New York Times*. Bookstores around the country are polled for the best-selling titles in their stores, and it is these data on which the list is based. And once you're on it, list-generated sales should keep you there for at least two or three more weeks.

Of course there's no way the *New York Times* could call each and every bookstore in the country every week to request information about their biggest selling books, so they have instead a small, closely-guarded list of bookstores that is thought to represent the American book-buying climate. The only problem with this idea is the ease with which it is corrupted. If one knows which stores these list-compilers call, he can buy enough of his own books to get listed. An article appeared in the British magazine *The Sunday Express* on May 7th, 1978 about Tony Curtis' novel *Kid Coty and Julie Sparrow*. According to the article, Curtis was given the opportunity to buy himself onto the Bestseller's List, at a price of about $15,000. This was over a decade ago, so the price has probably tripled by now. Apparently this is not an uncommon practice, and agents have been known to supply authors with a list of key spots to buy their own book in quantity.

Since many people are either too busy or too lazy to read, more and more books are making their way to audio cassettes. And since self-publishers want their books on tape too, several companies have sprung up to offer this service to fledgling authors. Crystal Audio Publishing and American Audio Literature will record, package, and internationally distribute your book-on-tape for a fee and/or a percentage of the royalties. Write them for free information about their services.

> **Crystal Audio Publishing**
> P.O. Box 210307
> Bedford, TX 76095
>
> **Amer. Audio Literature**
> P.O. Box 392
> Cicero, NY 13039

The cheapest, quickest and sneakiest way to become a full-fledged author is through microfiche. After you've typed up your manuscript, look under "Microfiche Services" in the Business-to-Business Yellow Pages of the nearest large city. You'll find a number of companies willing to create a master microfiche of your "book" and make about 100 copies for a grand total of about $50. Publishing your book via microfiche allows you to copyright your work, get an ISBN number and be listed in "Books In Print", the treatment afforded traditional books. Microfiche is a big thing with libraries, so you can distribute your book to every major public library in the state for just a few dollars.

Poet

Much of the foregoing on becoming a published author also applies to becoming a published poet, but there are two additional possibilities to explore here.

First, there are the anthology companies whose business is to compile collections of poems from aspiring poets desiring to see their name in print. Subscribers to these books will conveniently have one poem each printed in them. These anthologies cost between $10 and $30, and really aren't a bad deal for people who just want to see their work on the printed page. Anthology companies advertise heavily in *Writer's Digest*, or you can write these reputable publishing houses at left.

> **National Library of Poetry**
> **5-E Gwynns Mill Court**
> **Owings Mills, MD 21117**
>
> **Quill Books**
> **P.O. Box 728**
> **Minot, ND 58702**

Another way of gaining exposure as a poet is to blitzkrieg. Submitting your work to every listing in *Poet's Market* ($20 in most bookstores), every contest in *Writer's Digest*, and every literary magazine should get it published somewhere. And who knows, you might even get paid for it.

Songwriter

In the competitive music business, rarely does an unknown sell his or her lyrics to a large recording company. These industry giants will be the first to admit that there is some real talent out there in the amateur ranks, but they simply cannot afford to wade through the swamp and take unnecessary risks in such a high-stakes game.

CRS Records, however, will at least take a look at your lyrics. They are much more liberal in their acceptance policy and they actually prefer to work with new talent.

> **CRS Records**
> **Songwriting Dept.**
> **Box 814**
> **Lewiston, NY 14092**

If they feel your work has any semblance of potential in today's market, they are very likely to offer you a recording contract.

If you just want a few tapes or records to distribute to friends or local radio stations, you can send your rock, gospel or rap lyrics to Gude Studios. For only $79.95, they will produce a tape with your words set to their original melody. The song will then be owned 50/50 by you and Gude. A less expensive route would be to send your words to an independent songwriter who has his own studio. David Bultman is one such songwriter who advertises in various national music magazines and will develop a tune, record the song on cassette, and return it to you in about two weeks. Total cost: about $45. Either way, write to these people first before sending lyrics or money.

> Gude Studios
> P.O. Box 2861
> Burlington, NC
>   27216
>
> David Bultman
> 526 Hawthorne Dr.
> Omro, WI 54963

If you've got the words and the right tune, you can easily produce or "cut" a record yourself. And if you're willing to supervise the entire procedure, you can really save a bundle. You must get *The Complete Guide to Independent Recording: How to Make and Sell Your Own Record.* This comprehensive resource book, which sells for $16.95, is the bible of the independent recording industry, and the revised edition even shows how to get your tunes on Compact Discs. Available from Jerome Headlands Press, Perigee Books, or through inter-library loan.

> Jerome Headlands
> P.O. Box N
> Jerome, AZ 86331
>
> Perigee Books
> Putnam Pub. Group
> 200 Madison Ave.
> New York, NY 10016

Movie Star

Although maybe not with money, aspiring starlets have been buying their way into films for decades. The casting couch is an institution in Tinsel Town and is very likely to remain so. It's not exactly relevant for us though, since we want to be immortalized on celluloid the easy way: by paying for it. And if you have enough money, there are quite a number of options open to you.

First, you can make your own movie, and like Kevin Costner in "Dances With Wolves," cast yourself in the lead. This isn't very practical for most of us, so we may have to settle for a bit part in someone else's film. Bit parts, which require the actor or actress to say only a sentence or two, or appear in several scenes, do not require Olivier-like acting skills, and are not at all impossible for the clever status-seeker to arrange.

Bit parts and other minor movie roles are often advertised for in the trade publications at right. Send a few dollars for a sample copy of the magazines you are interested in. When you find something of interest, you can send your photo and resume, but remember, you'll be competing against hundreds of other would-be actors.

Backstage Productions
330 W. 42nd St.
16th Floor
New York, NY 10036

Commercials Monthly
470 S. San Vincente
Suite 103
Los Angeles, CA 90048

Daily Variety
1400 N. Cahuenga Blvd.
Hollywood, CA 90027

Drama-Logue
P.O. Box 38771
Los Angeles, CA 90038

On Valentines Day, 1990, one of the items available at a charity auction held at Christie's in New York was a small part in an upcoming Woody Allen movie. We're beginning to see such things more and more frequently, as film stars and other celebrities feel the need to become spokespersons for one charity or another. A good way to find these auctions is by writing major auction houses directly, particularly those on the west coast. Also, you can browse through *Town & Country* magazine, which occasionally lists such events each month in its "Chronicle" section. Christie's did not disclose the winning bid, but this is probably an expensive route to stardom.

Walk-ons and extras are always in demand, and these parts require no qualifications other than having the right look, and the ability to show up on the set. Once in A Lifetime has connections in the movie industry and can occasionally arrange for you to appear in an upcoming motion picture. The parts they arrange most often are of the "innocent bystander" or "dead soldier" variety, but every now and then can manage a minor speaking role for a couple hundred dollars. They offer a booklet which describes all their services, and I strongly suggest you order it. It's only $5, and is quite an interesting read.

> Once In A Lifetime
> 9205 SE Clackamas Road
> Suite #419
> Clackamas, OR 97015

Just as the book publishing industry has subsidy publishers, the motion picture industry has followed suit with at least one subsidy movie company. For a flat fee, you can take part in the production of a feature film. If you're a student director with a desire to take part in a big production, an aspiring actor who wants to add to your credits, or just a film buff who has always wanted to be in a movie, Charter Films can make your dream come true. Your first step should be to request their handbook, *The Charter Films Motion Picture Participation Manual*, which costs $20 postpaid.

> Charter Films
> 3119 Isabel Drive
> Los Ang., CA 90065

Conductor

Anyone who has ever wanted to conduct a real live orchestra, instead of waving an imaginary baton at the stereo, can now realize this dream thanks to Experientia, Ltd. For a $600 tax-deductible donation, one will receive a conducting lesson, an autographed copy of the score that is played, and a photo of you, the conductor, leading the San Diego Symphony Orchestra. Or, for a $1,000 donation, you can conduct the 26-piece Minneapolis Chamber Symphony located in St. Paul. You can also retain the Symphony and conduct them at your own private party for an additional $3,000.

> **Experientia, Ltd.**
> **419 N. Larchmont**
> **Suite 97**
> **Los Ang., CA 90004**

MONEY OCCUPATIONS

Bank President

It is possible to start your own bank without a great deal of capital, yet enjoy all the privileges that the occupation of bank president entails. The first method would be to start not a bank, but a credit union. Don't let this throw you - credit unions are empowered to do most of what a full-service bank can do: loan money, issue credit cards, and open checking and savings accounts.

There are a few picky regulations one must follow, but all you really need for the initial start-up is seven people for the Board of Directors (you and your six closest friends) and 200 more people willing to invest in the credit union. For more information, write the National Credit Union Administration and ask for the address of the regional office that serves your area. Once you contact the regional office, ask

> **National Credit**
> **Union Admin.**
> **Information Dept.**
> **Wash., DC 20456**

for complete guidelines for the formation of a credit union. It really is easier than one might think.

Another method for becoming a bank president is buying your own. I know you're saying, "Yeah, right," but you may be surprised just how easily and cheaply a bank can be purchased off-shore. If this is something you'd like to explore, Queensgate Associates offers a consultancy service for those thinking of taking the off-shore plunge. The cost for a detailed, customized report is $100, and once they ascertain what it is precisely you are looking for, it takes about 2-4 weeks worth of research.

> **Queensgate Associates**
> **National House - M**
> **Santon, Isle of Man**
> **British Isles (UK)**

CEO

Chief Executive Officer. It sounds pretty prestigious, but it doesn't take much effort to become one. You need only form your own corporation and declare yourself CEO. Northstar Corporate Services can set you up a no-frills corporation for only $150, and since your company can be officially headquartered in Delaware, there are no corporate taxes levied. Laughlin Associates, located in tax-free Nevada, offers a complete package, with stock certificates, corporate seal, and the works for $595. Both of these companies can perform their services through the mail and the complete process only takes about a week.

> **Northstar Corporate Svcs.**
> **134 State Street**
> **Albany, NY 12207**
>
> **Laughlin and Associates**
> **1000 E. William St. #100**
> **Carson City, NV 89701**

Ready-made foreign companies are available for $200 and up, and you can be a CEO of a corporation headquartered in such exotic locations as Liberia, Western Samoa or

Panama, without leaving the U.S. Having business cards printed with your international company is a great status booster, particularly at cocktail parties or other snobbish get-together. Below are some agents who can arrange these bargain off-shore companies.

Colin Forster Overseas Co. Registration Companies House Ransey, Isle of Man, UK	Diana Bean 24 Raffles Place 26-05 Clifford Ctr. Singapore 0104
Kevin Mirecki 2121 Ave. of the Stars 6th Floor Los Angeles, CA 90067	Peter Sidney 72 New Bond Street London W1Y 9DD England

Insurance Agent

You probably think that the occupation of insurance salesman is hardly appropriate for a list concerned with prestigious occupations, but there is one exception to this generalization. Becoming a partner or "name" at Lloyd's of London, the famed insurance underwriter, is a highly sought-after position. Scope Books sells a book called *The Lloyd's Report* which explains the complete procedure for obtaining a partnership in this elite organization. There is no work to do and no investment required, but your income should be between $50,000 and $250,000 for the rest of your life if you qualify. The book is $130 plus postage.

> Scope Books, Ltd.
> 62 Murray Road
> Horndean, Hants.
> PO8 9JL
> Great Britain

Attorney

No, you can't actually buy your way into the legal profession, but there is a shortcut worth mentioning. In California, there are several colleges of law that teach exlusively by correspondence courses. These colleges are licensed by the state, and graduates are entitled to take the California Bar Exam. These programs usually take less time, and are much less expensive than traditional law school. Two such schools are:

Newport University College of Law 3720 Campus Drive Newport Beach CA 92660	N. Western Calif. Univ. School of Law 1750 Howe Ave. #535 Sacramento CA 95825

POWER OCCUPATIONS

Government Posts

If you donate enough money to the election campaign of a presidential or gubernatorial candidate, and your candidate wins, you may just be rewarded with an appointment to a high-ranking government post. Although we're talking several thousand dollars here, this is one tried and true method of getting an all-title-no-work position.

A cheaper and perhaps more direct way is to peruse the government publication *Guide to Support Positions* which can be found at any large university library in the Federal Depository section. This book, known in Washington as the "plum book," is a complete list of easy government positions, or "plums," which by law must be given to a civilian over a politician, if the civilian is more qualified. Sounds fair to me.

Diplomat

If you have a clean criminal record, and more importantly, plenty of cash, you can become an honorary consul, attache, or even an ambassador to or from a Third World country. There are several well-connected agencies that can, for the right price, arrange these appointments for you. The cheapest of these is the honorary consulship, which is becoming so popular among well-heeled businessmen, the *Wall Street Journal* ran an article on the perks of these positions. In theory, these honorary diplomats have some of the responsibilities and privileges as regular career diplomats, but they don't get paid and few are ever called upon to do much work. Mostly, they just go to parties. Dan London, honorary consul-general for the Republic of Ceylon to San Francisco, says he gets about 40 diplomatic invitations per year, a bonanza of networking possibilities.

The compensation for this arduous profession comes mainly in prestige to be sure, but honorary diplomats get "consular corps" license plates, just like their career counterparts, so fending off the occasional parking and traffic ticket seems to be an added bonus. The biggest expense of being an honorary consul seems to be reciprocating with parties of your own and entertaining visiting dignitaries.

Below are some agencies that I've personally checked out, and feel good about recommending. I believe these people to be honest and forthright, and very seious about what they do. Be that as it may, *caveat emptor*.

Financial Engineering Consultants appears to be quite well-connected in Central and South America, and have been successful in arranging honorary consulates in Panama and a few other countries. They are now negotiating with leaders of other nations, and should be able to offer a larger selection of honoraries in the near future. Send them $20 for their information packet.

**F.E.C., Inc.
Box 959, Centro
Colon 1007
San Jose
Costa Rica**

One of the more professional and discreet organizations

in this field is SDG, a firm located in Porza, Switzerland. This company is composed of individuals who specialize in providing diplomatic posts and a host of other services to the well-to-do. They apparently have connections with high-level international attorneys and can perform some astonishing deeds. Usually these appointments are from smaller countries to western countries, like the US or Canada, and are, generally speaking, for life.

Here's one of their honorary consulship deals: SDG takes an up-front fee of $15,000, $13,000 of which is placed in an escrow account. Their handbook of step-by-step instructions is mailed to you, and a short meeting is arranged in Europe (or anywhere else if you pay for transportation) so that a detailed plan may be drawn up. If, after reviewing their handbook, you want to proceed on your own, withdraw or change your mind before the personal conference, you get a refund of the $13,000. This puts only $2,000 of your money at risk. After the meeting, however, there can be no refund since they will have invested alot of time and effort and divulged highly-confidential information. Once the process starts, you will not be reimbursed unless they are unable to secure your desired appointment within two years. According to SDG, this has never happened.

Prices for their other posts and services range from $500 to over $1,000,000 and they are so matter-of-factly direct, you'd think they were selling furniture. Their catalog, which is published twice annually, carries a price of $50 to "discourage curiosity seekers and to keep the riff-raff away."

> **SDG**
> **Sercoex SA**
> **via Cantonale 42**
> **Ch-6948 Porza**
> **Switzerland**

Another nifty buy in diplomatic credentials comes from the Knights of Malta, mentioned in the last chapter. The sovereignty of this order is recognized by about 30 countries on a de facto basis, so with all this clout, it is amazing that one can obtain a diplomatic passport from the order for about $2,900. With these diplomatic credentials, and a bit of a brassy attitude, one can receive all manner of privileges, and the prestige that accompanies this position is immeasurable.

> **Knights of Malta**
> **Hospitallers House**
> **London, England**
> **WC1N 3XX (UK)**

There's an interesting book distributed by GRF Press entitled *Above The Law: The Complete Guide to Obtaining Diplomatic Immunity*. Although the slant of the book is a bit different, there are specific suggestions given for the procurement of diplomatic appointments, and a number of sources are given in the Appendix. The book costs $19.95 postpaid.

> **GRF Press**
> **2050 Idle Hour Ctr.**
> **Suite #108**
> **Lexington, KY 40502**

And finally, there's an interesting and inexpensive possibility in receiving diplomatic appointments from the Baronial Order of St. Lawrence. This chivalrous organization has as its short-term goal the accreditation of ambassadors to every American state, Canadian province and foreign country, and consuls to every large city. You will receive your letters patent, diplomatic credentials, auto sticker and, of course, an ambassadorial sash for formal occasions. You'll want to write first to make sure your area is available. Total cost for an ambassadorship is $250, while consulships can be had for as little as $50.

> **Baronial Order of**
> **St. Lawrence**
> **8177 S. Harvard**
> **Suite #202**
> **Tulsa, OK 74137**

Head of State

If you'd rather run a country than merely represent one, and don't want the worrisome headaches of running for office, you can start your own. Seriously. Several ambitious entrepreneurs have undertaken the ultimate enterprise: the formation of an actual sovereign nation.

Among the most successful new countries have been the Principality of Sealand, the Sultanate of Occusi-Ambeno, and the Principality of Castellania. Some are run more or less as a hobby - like a model railroad - issuing stamps and passports, minting coins, etc., but others are very serious about achieving traditional recognition.

Prince Roy, the monarch of Sealand, claimed a WW2 aircraft tower off the coast of England and declared it an independent state. He has even engaged in a minor war with Germans in order to protect the territorial waters of his "country." Castellania is run by Prince Ralph I, who searched the charts of the globe for unclaimed territory, and found a stretch of sand that remains submerged in all but low tide. He has not disclosed the exact location of Castellania, for fear that it will suddenly be annexed by some existing nation. The Principality has several commercial representatives around the world who distribute publicity materials and citizenship applications.

For further information on forming your own nation, get the aptly titled *How to Start Your Own Country* by Erwin S. Strauss. Strauss is a controversial author who also wrote a book called *Basement Nukes,* which explains how to build your own atomic bomb. The only problem, of course, is getting the Uranium. These and other useful texts are available from Loompanics Unlimited. Send $5 for their latest catalog and future seasonal supplements.

Loompanics Unlimited
P.O. Box 1197
Port Townsend, WA
98368

ADVENTURE OCCUPATIONS

Fighter Pilot

For $10,000, you can experience all your "Top Gun" fantasies (provided they do not involve Tom Cruise or Kelly McGillis) thanks to Dreams Come True, a Los Angeles based firm. Go for the ride of your life in a real fighter jet, going from zero to 37,000 feet straight up in less than a minute, with a 720-degree roll thrown in for good measure. The price includes travel to and from LA. If this is a bit much, you can actually *fly* a Lear jet along the southern California coastline. The flight includes gourmet treats, and you can bring up to five friends along for the ride. This adventure is sponsored by Experientia, Ltd., and costs about $1,700 all inclusive.

> **Dreams Come True**
> John Alexander Assoc.
> 2753 Glendower Ave.
> L. A., CA 90027
>
> **Experientia, Ltd.**
> 419 Larchmont Blvd.
> Suite 97
> L.A., CA 90004

Racecar Driver

Experientia, Ltd. can also set you up behind the wheel of a Formula 2000 racer. These single seat, mid-engine open-wheel racing machines are equipped with front and rear stabilizer wings and are capable of rocketing to 100 Km/h in under five seconds. After a classroom session, each student is fitted with his own Formula 2000, where the morning is spent behind the wheel enjoying exercises in preparation for the afternoon lapping. Top professional drivers will share their secrets of driving to the limit to round out the day. The cost of this package is only $500, but a day of private, personal instruction with the track all to yourself can be arranged for about $3,500.

Reporter

Members of the press somehow manage to gain access to the insider events - the parties, the meetings, the crime scenes - from which the rest of us, it seems, is excluded. Is there some magic invitation that allows them entry into this secret world? As a matter of fact, there is - and it's called the press pass. With such a pass, one is invited to sit on the sidelines of a major sporting event, interview foreign dignitaries, and chit chat with celebrities. And yes, as you've probably guessed by now, there is a way that you can buy this wonderful document.

The most prestigious press pass available for a price is from *International Photographer Magazine*, the publication of the International Freelance Photographers Organization. A lifetime membership to IFPO costs about $35, and this entitles you to buy a cornucopia of press paraphernalia. Although they don't have any of those hat cards Clark Kent made so fashionable, their catalog contains passes, badges, windbreakers, dash cards, luggage tags, and everything else you can write "PRESS" on.

The reason IFPO is so useful is because they will write an assignment request to the publicity or security department of an event you want to cover, which virtually guarantees your acceptance, and occasionally results in backstage passes and special invitations. Write for a free sample issue of *International Photographer*, which contains full particulars on how to join.

IFPO
P.O. Box 18205
Wash., DC 20036

Detective

Thanks to Magnum, PI, Sam Spade and other fictional detectives, there is a very appealing mystique surrounding the private investigator. Actually, becoming a licensed detective is not very difficult, and some states have no licensing requirements at all. To discover the current procedure in your state, you can send for *Obtaining You P.I. License* printed by Orion Agency, and available for a few dollars from Paladin Press.

> **Paladin Press**
> **P.O. Box 1307**
> **Boulder, CO 80306**

There are two detective training schools that teach via correspondence, and one need never leave the comfort of their easy chair to learn all there is to know about undercover work.

> **Global School**
> **P.O. Box 191**
> **Hanover, MA 02339**
>
> **Rouse School**
> **P.O. Box 2469**
> **Costa Mesa, CA 92626**

Rouse also offers graduates a catalog of badges and identification, and plenty of gadgets to get you into loads of trouble. The cost for each of these courses is about $300.

Spy

As strange as it may sound, men have been using this bit to pick up women since "Goldfinger," and it still seems to be a viable routine. There's no overt status to be gained here, since posing as a secret agent requires you to convince other people you are in the espionage business without letting them know you know they know. Actually, it sounds more complicated than it is. A few strategically "hidden" CIA manuals, foreign passports and some sophisticated eavesdropping gadgets should do the trick.

How does one come by all these cloak-and-dagger toys? Loompanics Unlimited, arguably the best book catalog in the world, sells reprints of CIA and other government manuals as well as books on lock-picking, beating burglar alarms,

> **Loompanics**
> **P.O. Box 1197**
> **Pt. Town., WA 98368**

safecracking, overthrowing governments - you name it. Their latest catalog is available for $5.

As for electronic gadgets, PK Electronic sells auto-tailing devices, miniature transmitters, infra-red viewers, mini watch cameras, and enough other high-tech equipment to make James Bond envious. Write them for information about their latest catalog, which costs about $50 or so.

**PK Electronic
Heidenkampsweg 74
2000 Hamburg 1
Germany**

Chapter Four: Weird Credentials For Sale

There are several other documents and credentials that one may purchase and they are lumped together here in a separate chapter. The bulk of these credentials sellers concentrate on military or business-related IDs, but there are some good all-purpose credentials to be had as well.

Docugraphics bills itself as a "document replacement center" and appears to cater to the James Bond wanna-be's of the world. Aside from CIA service citations and Navy SEALS certificates, they also have a few college degrees and some miscellaneous other awards available. These certificates are about $8 each.

Docugraphics
3232 SW 34 Blvd.
Suite 115
G-ville, FL 32608

NIC offers most of the stuff Docugraphics sells, plus about a thousand more of their own. Particularly impressive are the International Drivers License, the Tax-Exempt ID Card, and the Concealed Weapons Permit. Their catalog is a trip into soldier-of-fortuneville, and some of their IDs are a real treat to read. The Federal Internal Bureau's card, for example, reads, "Remember that the agent knows best and is here to help you. Take off your clothes and follow the agent's instructions exactly." Hmmm... Since this is among NIC's best sellers, you can't help but wonder how many patriotic young ladies have unwittingly fallen for this ruse. NIC's cards are arranged so that the buyer affixes his own photo, then laminates it. They cost about $5 each.

NIC, Inc.
220 Carroll St., Suite D
P.O. Box 5950
Shreveport, LA 71135

Big Bear Press sells photo ID cards for supervisors, sales

representatives, general managers, employees, counselors, and a few more miscellaneous business-related IDs. These cards are only $1 each, but again, you must type the personal information yourself, attach a photo, then laminate it.

> **Big Bear Press**
> **555 Saturn Blvd.**
> **Suite B-430**
> **San Diego, CA 92154**

For only $5, World Enterprises will make you a Regional Vice-President, or at least supply you with credentials identifying you as such. The card itself is rather amateur in appearance though, and would probably not fool anyone worth fooling.

> **World Enterprises**
> **3909 E. Semoran Blvd.**
> **Apopka, FL 32703**

On the other hand, Global Industries International's ID card is very impressive. It looks like a high-security passkey, and identifies you as being Executive Vice-President, with total security clearance. Exactly what you gain clearance to is another matter altogether. The catch, however, is that the credentials kit costs $30.

> **Global Industries Int'l**
> **9925 Lyndale Ave. S**
> **Suite 205**
> **Bloomington, MN 55420**

Delta Insignia specializes in military badges, medals, and patches, and supplied the Soviet insignia for the Paramount film, "Hunt For Red October."

> **Delta Insignia**
> **215 S. Washington**
> **P.O. Box 1565**
> **El Dorado, AR 71731**

Ideal Studios offers blank birth certificates, licenses for private, commercial or helicopter pilots, and even motor vehicle bills of sale. This company has been in business for quite a few years,

> **Ideal Studios**
> **P.O. Box 41156**
> **Chicago, IL 60641**

and frankly, I'm amazed that they have managed to stay out of legal trouble that long.

Music photographer Lynn Goldsmith has developed a line of look-alike concert passes called "Backstage Counterfeits." These controversial laminated passes are so authentic-looking, they have been called a security risk by the industry. Although Goldsmith's company, ICONS, advertises the backstage passes as counterfeit, they have confused many security staffs, and have allowed kids to gain complete access to their favorite musical stars. This isn't exactly new. Concert-goers are notorious for cutting out sections of cassette covers, using press-on transfer letters to write "BACKSTAGE" on them, laminating the cover, then tying it around their neck with lanyards. Backstage Counterfeits will be available in music stores for $4.99 by late 1992. For those interested in receiving real backstage passes, see Chapter Nine.

CSA Printing House markets a passport of the Confederate States of America. "This passport," according to their literature, "is not valid for identification, and is sold for the sole purpose of exciting interest in this unique aspect of American history."

**CSA Printing House
P.O. Box 60
Whitestone, NY 11357**

The Baird Company sells novelty credentials of a mostly humorous nature. ID cards are available for such illustrious positions as Fighter Pilot, Gun For Hire, and Amateur Gynecologist, which identifies one as being "authorized to practice on all who is willing till he gits (sic) it right."

**Baird Company
P.O. Box 444
Los Alamitos CA
90720**

Undoubtedly the most interesting entry in this chapter is an organization called the International Awards Committee. Apparently, the IAC's main function is to bestow awards, honors and credentials upon its benefactors, and verify inquiries that anyone investigating these credentials may have. After all, if you are going to include an honorary award on a resume, you'd better be able to back up such a claim.

IAC offers several dozen "stock" awards for about $90 each, and once someone purchases one, they will not be given to anyone else. Some of these stock awards are listed below, and with every purchase, one receives unlimited verification on all inquiries. For $145, they will custom design and bestow the honorary of your choosing, as long as there exists no actual award of that particular designation. (Sorry to disappoint all those nobel laureate hopefuls out there.) The International Award Committee offers several additional services which may be of interest, such as backdating awards, issuing press releases to local newspapers, etc. Write for their brochure, which at press time cost $5.

> **Int'l Award Committee**
> **Sercoex SA**
> **via Cantonale 42**
> **CH-6948 Porza**
> **Switzerland**

> Ogilvy Fellowship
> Man of the Year
> Woman of the Year
> Willowdale Prize
> Entrepreneurial Award
> Bleckner Science Prize
> Garrand Scholarship
> Pella Citation
> Oxbridge Award
> Memling Prize
> Haversham Honorary
> Outstanding Student
> Humanitarian Award

Chapter Five:
A Day In The Life of A Status Symbol Master

We've spent alot of time in the previous chapters dealing with status symbols of an intangible, non-physical nature. While these are of extreme value, the most famous and overtly admired status symbols are the good old-fashion trinkets and toys of the rich and famous.

The purchase of such trappings, which Thorstein Veblen labeled "conspicuous consumption" in *Theory of the Leisure Class*, is almost universal among the well-to-do, and these toys include mansions, yachts, fast cars, expensive jewelry, and other quintessential status symbols. While I would love to give you a list of places where yachts and Beverly Hills mansions could be purchased inexpensively, there are, alas, none to offer. It seems that bargain hunters are often *persona non grata* in status symbol land.

I will relate here, however, a little story of one such bargain hunter - we will call her Judith - who can quite successfully accumulate a treasure trove of prestige at a moments notice, and without spending a great deal of money. Hopefully "Judith" will give you some inspiration and a few ideas you may implement in your own life.

Our story begins as Judith was telephoned one day by an old college acquaintance, Dolores Namedropper, who mentioned she would be in town for a few days and would love to get together again. Remembering Dolores as an arrogant, pretentious, status-conscious opportunist (or, as we say in the business, a snob), Judith knew Dolores' sole motive for "getting together" was to rub her new high-paying job and handsome fiancee in her face. But Judith agreed to have lunch the *next* day, allowing herself enough time to make the necessary arrangements.

When Dolores arrived at Judith's house, she was greeted at the door by a liveried butler. Actually, "Jeeves" was hired for the day from a local catering service, something that can be arranged in just about any city. Upon stepping into the foyer, she was immediately aware of Judith's multi-million dollar art collection. "Judith must have done very well for herself," Dolores thought, eyeing the original Monets and Renoirs on the wall. Well actually, Judith purchased these "originals" for about $300 each from one of the several firms now offering exact reproductions of art masterpieces. Thanks to new technological breakthroughs, these forgeries are virtually impossible to tell from the original works. They are painted on canvas, and have the exact same texture, pigments and brush strokes as the original. The most famous and reputable company providing this service is N.A. DeNunzio Co. Send $7 for their latest catalog.

> **N.A. DeNunzio Co.**
> **40 Scitico Road**
> **P.O. Box 508**
> **Somersville CT 06072**

Judith's impressive collection of statuary is again a group of nearly undetectable reproductions. Eleganza, Ltd. offers exact reproductions of famous sculptures, bronzes, ancient Greek vases, frieze fragments, etc., and their prices, starting at about $40 and peaking at over $4,000, reflect the eclectic nature of Eleganza's collection. An interesting aging process lends an air of authenticity to their products.

> **Eleganza, Ltd.**
> **3217 W. Smith St.**
> **Seattle, WA 98199**

The butler extended Judith's apologies for not being quite ready, so that Dolores could take the opportunity to snoop around a bit more. A surreptitious look into a nearby ice bucket revealed something rather peculiar. Pulling the empty bottle from the bucket, Dolores was perplexed; the wine seemed to have been from Judith's private vineyard. "Surely not," Dolores thought. Of course not! Last year, Judith had had some fancy labels printed, and whenever certain guests stop by, she simply attaches them to bottles of her favorite wine. (Luckily, I do not have to go to such extremes; Seagrams already distributes a wonderful Chateau de Montfort vouvray.)

When Judith finally entered the drawing room to give her old chum a hug, Dolores was made instantly aware of Judith's $300 per ounce perfume. Of course, Judith only paid about $30 an ounce for the exact chemical replica. Perfume counterfeits are available today for some rather prestigious brands, including L'Air du Temps (Princess Di's favorite), Joy (the perfume of both Princess Grace and Jacqueline Onassis) and a host of others. Although fake perfumes seem to be sold everywhere these days, some of the highest quantity are marketed by Paris Perfumes, which also produces a few perfumes of its own.

> **Paris Perfumes**
> **25 Aladdin Avenue**
> **Dumont, NJ 07628**

Dolores was also taken aback by Judith's incredible designer outfit. But don't think for a minute that Judith paid full price. No way. Discount clothing shops often sell expensive designer clothes at an extremely reduced rate because of a very minor flaw. The labels, however, are removed to prevent the customer from knowing who the designer is. This can easily be discovered by looking at the RN Number which, by law, must remain on the garment at all times. For a complete list of these numbers, you can order the *RN Directory* from Textile Publishing, which lists every clothing manufacturer today. But to get you started, here are some RN Numbers of the more famous designers:

> **Textile Publishing**
> **P.O. Box 50079**
> **Wash., DC 20013**

Bill Blass (RN38344)	Halston (41564, 46616, 53702)
Christian Dior (03005)	Anne Klein (40803)
Perry Ellis (57272)	Calvin Klein (41327, 42642)
Ralph Lauren (56158)	Gloria Vanderbilt (52130)

As they prepared to leave, Judith attached her fake beeper/pager, and volunteered to drive. After being led into the garage, Dolores almost fell to her knees in shock. She simply could not believe that Judith's car was a brand-new bright-red Lambourghini Countache. You should know by now that Judith had the car built from a replica kit, and got what looks like a $250,000 car for the price of a Hyundai.

> Fake Beepers:
> **All Electronics**
> **Box 567**
> **Van Nuys, CA 91408**

There are several manufacturers of Lambourghini clones, each with a different style (to avoid trademark and copyright suits) and price range. Some kits even come completely pre-built. Other prestige cars are available in kit form, and at left is a sampling of some companies that manufacture these counterfeit kit cars. You'll want to write them for the current price of their information package. For other companies not listed, check out *Kit Car* magazine, available at most large newsstands.

> Lambourghini:
> **Pace Motors**
> **P.O. Box 186**
> **Renton, WA 98057**
>
> **Elegant Motors, Inc.**
> **P.O. Box 30188**
> **Indianapolis, IN 46230**
>
> Ferrari:
> **Corson Motorcar Co.**
> **P.O. Box 41396**
> **Phoenix, AZ 85080**
>
> **Concept Automobiles**
> **1922 Old Mill Lane**
> **Henderson, NV 89014**
>
> Mercedes-Benz:
> **Thoroughbred Motors**
> **440 220th NE**
> **Redmond, WA 98053**

Dolores' attention was also drawn to the license plate on the front of the "Lambourghini," which read "JUDY-3." "Gee," Dolores thought, "if this is her *third* car, what must her other two be?" Who knows, but Johnson-Smith will print anything on their look-alike license plates, available for all 50 states, for only $23.

> **Johnson-Smith**
> P.O. Box 25500
> Bradenton, FL 34206

On the way to the restaurant, Judith activated her fake beeper and made a couple of phony, but oh-so-important-sounding phone calls on her phony car phone. These cute little imitation cellular phones look just like the real thing and even come with an antenna. They're available from Harriet Carter, the famous novelty distributor, for $6.98.

> **Harriet Carter**
> Dept. 10
> N. Wales, PA 19455

At the end of lunch, Judith demanded that she be allowed to pay. Dolores seized her chance and said, "Okay, but only if I can get dinner." So a foursome was planned for that evening and Dolores was ecstatic. Judith hadn't let her begin her presentation all day, and by golly, tonight she was going to show her the meaning of success. Judith readily accepted, though, for she knew she still had a few tricks up her sleeve.

With just the right amount of polished insouciance, Judith withdrew from her fake alligator wallet a VISA Gold Card and arranged it face up on the tray. When the waiter returned, she signed the receipt with her fake Montblanc pen.

> Fake Alligator Wallet:
> **Durham House**
> **561 Acorn Street**
> **Deer Park, NY 11729**
> Gold Card Arranged By:
> **CSC**
> **5430 Lynx Lane**
> **Columbia, MD 21044**
> Fake Montblanc Pen:
> **Haverhills**
> **131 Townsend Street**
> **San Fran., CA 94107**

Dolores' rented limousine pulled up at Judith's house at 7:00, and Dolores and her fiancee emerged in evening gown and tuxedo. Judith was prepared, though, and greeted them at the door in her $25,000 designer gown (a rental, of course) and strands of priceless jewels. Okay, the jewels were fakes, but no one could have known. Kenya Gems sells jewelry containing artificial diamonds so close to the originals, gemologists have to resort to electronic equipment to tell them from the real thing. When asked to tell the difference between a real diamond and one of the above-mentioned phonies, a jeweler friend of mine immediately picked the right one. "Wait a minute," I said, "how did you know?" "I didn't," he admitted, "but if that one [the fake] were real, it would be worth a fortune, and I know you don't have *that* kind of money!" Hardly a reliable means of authentication.

> **Kenya Gems**
> **Day & Frick, Inc.**
> **1760 N. Howard**
> **Phila., PA 19122**

For other precious gems, like sapphires, rubies, and emeralds, A. Andrew and Co., Ltd. of Hong Kong sells jewelry containing perfect counterfeits for a tiny fraction of the authentic gemstone price. Send for their free gigantic catalog.

> **A. Andrew & Co., Ltd.**
> **38-44 D'Aguilar Street**
> **1/F**
> **(GPO Box 2983)**
> **HONG KONG**

Judith glanced at her fake Rolex, apologizing for the tardiness of her boyfriend and added, "You know how actors are." Soon Judith's "boyfriend" pulled into the driveway, and Dolores was amazed. Hadn't she seen him on television or in the movies somwhere? Probably. Judith's escort had appeared in several movies and a television series or two, and was now playing the part of "long-time boyfriend goes to dinner." Some of the more upscale escort services can provide movie stars, models and VIPs to accompany you to a party, dinner or other social

> **E.D.I.**
> **Box 464027**
> **Law'ville, GA 30246**

function at reasonable rates. On the West Coast, contact World Club at (800) 722-0050, and on the East Coast, the most prestigious escort agency is International Escorts in New York. There are escort services in most cities, but these are simply thinly disguised brothels. I'd advise sticking with the more reputable firms if status is what you're after.

> **Internat'l Escorts**
> **330 W. 56th St.**
> **NY, NY 10019**

Once In A Lifetime can also arrange a dinner date with a famous Hollywood star for prices starting at about $1,000. Send for their booklet, which explains who is available and for how much. The price of the book is $5.

> **Once In A Lifetime**
> **9205 SE Clackamas Rd.**
> **Suite 419**
> **Clackamas, OR 97015**

Judith threw on her artificial mink coat, which are now available everywhere, and away they went. This was the moment Dolores had been waiting for and she wasted no time in spinning her boastful, name-dropping tale of how wonderful she, her fiancee, and all their friends actually are. Judith listened intently, interjecting with the occasional "hmmm" and "aha," but all the while waiting for the upcoming *coup de grace*.

After everyone had finished with dinner, Dolores' fiancee reached for the bill, but was stopped short by the waiter. Turning to Judith's "boyfriend," the waiter said, "The owner has asked me to tell you that he loved your performance in 'The Godfather' and it would give him great pleasure if you and your party would accept this dinner as a gift of the restaurant."

Dolores was livid. On the way out, Judith surreptitiously slipped the waiter her credit card and his promised tip of $50. Dolores and her fiancee were never heard from again.

Chapter Six: Prestigious Addresses

Wouldn't it be nice if you could use a Beverly Hills or French Riviera address as your own without leaving the comfort of Boise or Memphis or wherever else you happen to live? Well you can, thanks to a wonderful invention called the mail-forwarding service.

A mail-forwarding service, or mail drop as they're called, allows you to use their office as your new address with no one the wiser. For example, if they are located at 500 Main Street, Anytown, USA, your address would be something like John Q. Reader, 500 Main Street, Suite #23, Anytown, USA. The mail drop would then know to put all letters coming in addressed with Suite 23 into a larger envelope, and mail them to where you actually live.

Not only is this great for status, but for privacy as well. In fact, several of the listings in this book are companies operating out of mail drops. (I checked.) But aren't their real addresses discovered when they have to mail something back? No, because mail-forwarding services also work in reverse. You can send them a package of letters to be mailed, which they post from their own office. This means any letter you send will have the mail drop's city postmark, so no one discovers your secret.

To find a mail drop in your target city, simply look in that city's Yellow Pages under "Mail Forwarding," or order *The 1992 Mail Drop Directory* from GRF Press. It contains a comprehensive list of mail-drops in the United States and abroad, and costs $10 postpaid.

> **GRF Press**
> **2050 Idle Hour Ctr**
> **Suite 108**
> **Lex'ton KY 40502**

Once you've contracted for this service, which is about

$10 per month, mail yourself a letter using the new address, and test the amount of time it takes to get back to you. And don't worry - mail-forwarding services live and die by their reputation for discretion and privacy, so you needn't fear their opening and reading your correspondence. Nor will they disclose whether or not you are a client unless forced to do so by a court order.

To get you started, here's a list of some mail drops at what many would consider prestige addresses. Before sending any money, write them for further information.

Mail Boxes, Etc.
22653 Pacific Coast Hwy.
Malibu, CA 90265

Mail Boxes, Etc.
3229 N Street NW
Washington, DC 20007

Concorde Communications
8530 Wilshire Blvd.
Beverly Hills, CA 90211

Princeton Mail Service
301 N. Harrison Street
Princeton, NJ 08540

Mail Boxes, Etc. USA
9016 Wilshire Blvd.
Beverly Hills, 90211

Mail Boxes, Etc.
351-B Pleasant Street
Northampton, MA 01060

United CA Mailbox Svc.
1770 N. Highland Ave. #H
Hollywood, CA 90028

Marshall Business Services
234 Fifth Avenue
New York, NY 10001

A-OK Business Services
350 Ward Ave. #106
Honolulu, HI 96814

Mail Boxes, Etc.
175 Fifth Avenue
New York, NY 10001

Mail Boxes, Etc. USA
Trafalgar Shopping Ctr.
6342 Forest Hills Blvd.
West Palm Beach, FL 33415

Royal Enterprises
114-41 Queens Boulevard
Suite #168
Forest Hills, NY 11375

Bette James & Associates
1439 Massachusettes Ave.
Cambridge, MA 02138

Mail Boxes, Etc. USA
18530 Mack Avenue
Grosse Pointe, MI 48236

Chapter Seven: Status While Traveling

Wherever the status-conscious may roam, they will always want to be treated with the proper respect and dignity, be seen in the "in" nightspots, and generally have the red carpet rolled out for them. Receiving this kind of treatment at home is not at all difficult, but being worshiped by total strangers requires a bit of planning. And, as with most other sections of this book, if you want to do it right, you'll need a little cash.

GETTING THERE

By far the quickest, and more importantly, most prestigious way to get from point A to point B is to fly. But as flying has become as commonplace as taking the subway, you'll need to check into the more luxurious modes of air travel.

Even before you board the plane, you can enjoy the luxury to which you are accustomed. Most airlines have VIP clubs, although each have their own name, which allow members to indulge themselves in a private lounge complete with antique furnishings, large screen TVs, free telephones, fax machines, a bartender and servants. It certainly beats waiting in those plastic coin-operated TV chairs from Hell. Contact the airline you fly most frequently for further details.

A number of nationwide discount ticketing agencies can arrange first class tickets around the world for up to 70% off the regular fare. Businessmen, for example, may have to cancel their flight at the last moment, so these discount ticket agencies buy up these tickets for pennies on the dollar. In some cases, you can even get First Class seats cheaper than Coach. These companies advertise heavily in the *Wall Street Journal.*

Flying the Concorde is, of course, the *creme-de-la-creme* of air travel. The price, however, at $8,000 for a round-trip flight, can be a bit prohibitive for many status-seekers. But thanks to an interesting courier program, you can travel supersonic at a much lower fare (currently $900 RT to London) and enjoy all the perks while sipping 20 year old whiskey at Mach 2. International Courier Travel is the sponsor of this deal, and they will send you complete details. But you'd better hurry before the fax machine all but does away with the courier business.

> **Int'l Courier Travel**
> **5757 W. Century**
> **Suite 700 - 26**
> **Los Ang., CA 90045**

Ordinarily, traveling by cruise ship would be a terribly expensive way to get to your destination, but thanks to some innovative "host" programs, you may be eligible to travel free of charge. To offset the disproportionate number of single women to single men aboard cruise ships, a couple cruise lines are offering certain "charming and gallant" men free tickets in exhange for their "entertaining" the single ladies aboard ship.

The inventor of this scheme, Royal Cruise Lines, says they currently have over 200 such hosts, but also add that they are very selective about whom they choose. Maybe so, but their host program brochure shows one of their "charming and gallant" men wearing - get this - a tan sports coat, a red-ruffled tuxedo shirt, and a black velvet bow tie. Yecchhh!

> **Royal Cruise Lines**
> **One Maritime Plaza**
> **San Fran., CA 94111**

Cunard Cruise Lines, owner of the Queen Elizabeth II, has a similar program, and full particulars may be obtained by writing them.

> **Cunard Cruises**
> **555 Fifth Avenue**
> **NY, NY 10017**

There are a few restrictions, especially age, but this may be your only chance to cross the ocean on the QE2 absolutely free.

ONCE YOU'RE THERE

After you've arrived, you will need a way to get about town, and for the red-carpeteer, subways and taxis simply won't do. There's always the limo, but that can be a tad vulgar on some trips. Several car rental agencies can now offer Ferraris (real ones), Rolls Royces and other nice automobiles. Sure they're a little more expensive than the regular sedan, but the prestige they convey certainly offsets the additional expense. A few American rental agencies also offer these ultra-luxury cars overseas. Contact the car rental agency you use most often before your trip. If they don't have the car you want, they will probably arrange to get it.

If this vacation takes you near water, you may want to go the whole nine yards and zip around the area in your own yacht. There's nothing quite like a 100' yacht to impress casual passers-by, and thanks to these yacht-chartering companies, you needn't worry about a large outlay of cash, nor trying to drive the darn thing.

Through the charter companies at right, yachts are available just about anywhere there is a major body of water, but if you're considering some of the more obscure vacationing spots, consult *Yachting* magazine (at newsstands everywhere) which usually contains dozens of yacht chartering advertisements.

Yacht Vacations World
P.O. Box 11179
St. Thomas, VI 00801

Bob Saxon Associates
1500 Cordova Rd #214
Ft. Lauder., FL 33316

Whitney Yacht Charters
2209 N. Halsted
Chicago, IL 60614

HOTEL AND RESTAURANT TRICKS

Restaurant and hotel employees are notoriously snooty, and sometimes simply do not possess the level of acquiescence that we status-seekers demand. However, there are a few tricks, tried and true, that make hotel clerks less hostile, turn restaurateurs into obsequious servants, and impress the hell out of your guests.

Before checking into a hotel, always have someone call several times and ask if you've arrived yet. If you have to do this yourself, change your voice each time. On the final call, say, "Will you have [you] call *People* (or *Time* or the *Wall Street Journal*, or whatever seems appropriate) when he/she arrives?" Now, call some of the most prestigious companies in the area you'll be visiting, and ask them some question that they will have to look into. Tell them when they get the answer, call you back at XYZ Hotel. When you finally do arrive to check in, and your fist-full of messages are delivered, casually flip through the notes, shake your head in mock disgust, and wad them up. You may also want to throw in a "I wish they would quit following me around wherever I go" or "Can't a fellow get some peace and quiet on vacation?" for good measure. As corny as this may sound, I know of two occasions where this resulted in a room full of flowers and several bottles of complimentary champagne. When they think you're somebody, they will treat you as such.

Another neat trick, which can be used in almost any situation where you need some quick, emergency status, is the old "hyphenation gambit." Find out the name of someone who's really important in the city, state or country you are visiting, and who also has a rather unusual surname. Then, whenever it's necessary to introduce yourself, throw this name in as a middle name or attach it to your own surname with a hyphen.

I know a lady who adopted the middle name "Cuomo"

while being admitted into a New York hospital. Every other minute someone asked, "Are you related to the governor?" And every time, she would answer, "Yes, but I don't want to be given any preferential treatment just because of Uncle Mario's position." Needless to say, she was given a great deal of preferential treatment. The possibilities of this kind of ruse are endless, and if used judiciously, will practically guarantee you royal treatment.

The same kind of tricks can be pulled at restaurants, and the results can be even more lucrative. Before making reservations, have someone call the restaurant and ask for the manager. Once the manager is on the line, have them lower their voice to a conspiratorial whisper and deliver the following monologue: "Hello [*Manager*], this is [*John Doe*] at [*Your Hotel*]. I just overheard [*Make Up A Name*], the restaurant critic for [*Any Magazine*] tell his/her assistant that he/she is planning to try your restaurant either tonight or tomorrow. I don't ordinarily do this, but I thought I'd just warn you. Oh, by the way, when [*Any Magazine*] left a message for [*Your Pseudonym*], they said to make reservations under the name of [*Your Real Name*]." When you finally arrive at the restaurant, you'd better believe you'll be treated like you own the place, and you might even get a complimentary meal out of the deal.

A variation on this is to look in the newspapers and see if anyone really famous is visiting, performing or passing through the area in which you're vacationing. Then, when you call to make reservations, say you would like to reserve a table for [*The Number In Your Party Plus One*] for [*Very Famous Person*] and [*Your Party*]. When you show up *sans* celebrity, you can just say that unfortunately they didn't feel like getting out tonight.

Other famous restaurant tricks, such as those mentioned in Chapter Five, require that you go to the restaurant in advance of your meal, and pay the waiter to say or do something nice. This will usually be something like: "It's so nice to see you again [*Your Name*]" or to come to your table at the middle of dinner to tell you you have a telephone call, or just whatever suits the occasion. I know one gentleman who has gone to a restaurant and paid for a bottle of their best champagne in advance. He then paid the waiter to come to the table at the end of dinner and say, "This is compliments of the restaurant for your outstanding contributions to humanity..."

If you're going to pull this kind of trick, it's best to approach employees when they are are out of view and earshot of their boss. Most employees will be glad to do whatever you want in order to pick up a generous tip, but owners and managers find it very unseemly. I can't imagine why.

GREAT SEATS

Usually, it takes some pretty good connections to arrange seats worthy of the professional social climber, but if your vacation includes attending a sporting event, concert or show, you are definitely going to need some good tickets. You can try your luck with scalpers, or you can contact SuperSeats. SuperSeats and other professional ticket agencies offer you not only good seats, but they sometimes have tickets available that are all but impossible to obtain. If you'd like to sit near the Royal Box at Wimbledon, in a clubhouse box at the Kentucky Derby, go backstage of a Broadway play and sit front-row center, you can write for their catalog or check out some of the ticket agencies that advertise daily in *USA Today*. SuperSeat's catalog is updated frequently, and each issue costs $5, or a year's subscription is available for $30.

> **SuperSeats**
> 8177 S. Harvard
> Suite 202
> Tulsa, OK 74137

THE PHONY HOLIDAY

In these status-conscious times, it may occasionally be advantageous to pretend that you're enjoying a prestigious vacation somewhere while actually holed-up in some cheap motel. The trappings of an actual vacation - postcards, souvenirs, a local newspaper - are easy to contrive, and you can always say you forgot your camera.

Souvenirs usually take the form of fun but useless little gifts, and What On Earth, an interesting company in Ohio, offers these things *en masse*. They have T-shirts and sweats from around the world, foreign language clocks and playing cards, and everything in between. The catalog has a $1 pricetag, but they will probably send you one free if you ask.

What On Earth
2451 Enterprise Pkwy
Twinsburg, OH 44087

Postcards are available from every state and just about every country from Foreign Cards, Ltd. Once you receive your cards, fill in your 'wish you were here' sentiments, and send them to a mail drop (see Chapter Six) for remailing. If the area you are visiting is not in GRF Press' mail drop directory, a call to that city's Directory Assistance might prove useful, especially since Mail Boxes, Etc. has a franchise in just about every medium-size city.

Foreign Cards, Ltd.
Box 123
Guilford, CT 06437

Multinewspapers, a California firm, will send you a sample or a subscription to almost any newspaper in the world, from Albania to Zimbabwe. The price for these papers is rarely over $5, and they always send the most current issue available.

Multinewspapers
Box DE
Dana Point, CA 92629

Chapter Eight: Fame and Immortality

I need hardly convince you of the benefits of fame and immortality. The ideas of being known and admired by all, or of being remembered long after we've departed this world, are attractive indeed. It's a pleasant dream for most of us - fantasizing about the autograph hounds, the world notoriety, and the "Hey aren't you..." recognition. And it's precisely these perks that make alot of people seek the limelight. But it's also nice to think that for years after we're gone, there will be monuments, both literally and figuratively, that remind future generations that not only did we exist, but had a real impact on the world.

It's no secret that these things can be bought. People have erected statues of themselves since time immemorial, and everyone knows how easy it is for a wealthy person to publicize themselves. But what about us, the not-so-wealthy? Are we relegated to relative obscurity without a chance to make a lasting impression on the future of our species? Absolutely not! There are many opportunities to buy fame and immortality - some cheap and some not. It really depends on your individual circumstances, but there are firms out there whose sole job is, regardless of your budget, to immortalize you for all time.

What follows is a beginner's list of such opportunities. The ideas here may act as catalysts to help you dream up your own plan. The listings here are in no particular order since what confers fame may very well offer some degree of immortality as well.

INSTANT EXPERT

When the Associated Press or CNN needs information on US population statistics or foreign policy, data are everywhere. In fact, with the right reference materials, you can find out everything from the mating patterns of llamas to the mechanics of dog-sledding. But when the media need a person to discuss a subject, or when they need to interview someone on a news program or for a newspaper article, where do they turn?

Most likely, they turn to the *Yearbook of Experts, Authorities and Spokespersons*. This annual guide is published by Broadcast Interview Source, and is subscribed to by every major media source in the world. Talk-show producers use the guide to find interesting guests who are required to intelligently discuss a certain topic, and newspaper and magazine reporters refer to the guide several times in the course of preparing in-depth articles. If you feel you merit the rank of "expert" in some area, you can be included in the next available issue of the guide for an inclusion rate of about $100 or so. And after being listed, don't be surprised to find the *New York Times* on the phone, or *60 Minutes* at your door.

> **Broadcast Interview**
> **2233 Wisconsin Ave.**
> **Suite #540**
> **Washington, DC 20007**

GETTING IN WHO'S WHO

There are many, many Who's Who-type books in the world, but none more prestigious than those published by Marquis' Who's Who, a division of MacMillan. *Who's Who in America* is the best known as well as the most prestigious of the nineteen directories Marquis publishes. Managing editor John Daniels says that *Who's Who in America*, which lists 80,000 distinguished Americans, accepts only about 400 write-in self-nominations each year, and he advises that this type of self-nomination causes Marquis to be a bit more cautious than usual.

The trick is to have someone already listed to write in and suggest that since you are so incredibly wonderful, the book really won't be complete until you're included. This is probably the most popular way of arranging to be listed, and if you don't know someone who can nominate you, there's a third, rather sneaky alternative.

A friend of mine once posed as a Who's Who listee, and vicariously nominated himself. He printed up phony stationery and wrote a grotesquely flattering letter about his many accomplishments. Apparently the real listee was never contacted to verify this nomination, so this man appeared in the next issue and is still there today.

Now obviously, Marquis motivation for publishing these books is not to be the international arbiter of VIP status, but to sell these books to libraries and those listed. Knowing this, a promise to buy future copies will probably carry as much weight toward acceptance as a Harvard PhD.

> **Marquis' Who's Who**
> **3002 Glenview Road**
> **Wilmette, IL 60091**

Likewise, social registers are a sort of Who's Who of the socially prominent, and care far more about family history than actual personal achievement. Each large city has its own, and invitations for inclusion can be rather tough to garner. Remember Chapter One's advice about moving up socially by moving physically? However, there is a group that is compiling a sort of worldwide social registry, and getting listed does not appear to be beyond the reach of the clever social climber. This book will probably become the equivalent of *Debrett's Peerage*, so getting listed is definitely something worth considering. The best part is, their primary motivation for this endeavor is to make money, so if you were to attach a check for the next three issues ($297) to your request for inclusion, stating very clearly that the check is to be cashed ONLY if you

> **Int'l Social Directory**
> **Block O Flat 3, Lily St.**
> **Neighborhood 2**
> **Sta. Lucia, MALTA**

are accepted. This will definitely get you in. I know; I tried.

BEST DRESSED LISTS

Unless you've really got serious money to spend, your odds of making a national "best dressed" list are almost nil. The secret is that there is no secret at all. All you must do is buy original dresses and gowns, or if you're a man, custom suits from the top ten designers, and be seen in them at important events with lots of media coverage.

Undoubtedly, the most influential of these lists is the one prepared by Mr. Blackwell, the merciless fashion critic. Although you cannot buy your way onto his best dressed list, you can certainly buy your way off his "worst dressed" list. Thanks to Experientia, Ltd., you can hire Mr. Blackwell as your very own fashion consultant. For $3,499, you get a full day of limousine chauffered shopping with the legendary Mr. Blackwell as your guide. Lunch and a $500 travel credit is included in the package.

> **Experientia, Ltd.**
> **419 Larchmont Blvd.**
> **Suite 97**
> **Los Angeles, CA 90004**

BEAUTY CONTESTOLOGY

The science of beauty contestology has a logic that is rather easy to follow: the more contests you enter, the more likely you are to win. Models and actresses can certainly improve a resume with a Miss Texas title, but so can any woman who wants to succeed in a public-oriented occupation.

> **World Pageants, Inc.**
> **10540 NW 26th St.**
> **Suite 304**
> **Miami, FL 33172**

World Pageants, Inc. publishes the *International Directory of Pageants*, which lists over 3,000 beauty contests worldwide each year. The directory, which sells for about $50, lists all the qualifications, dates, entry requirements, methods of judging, prizes, and everything else one needs to know to utilize the "volume" method. The book does not give the amount of bribes necessary to insure your win in the respective pageants, so this must be worked out on your own.

FAME FOR SALE

There are a number of companies that have the connections to get you on radio and television, in newspapers and magazines, and will gladly make your name a household word... for the right price. Your first choice might be to hire a publicist. These people have the contacts to get you on most national talk shows, news programs and in influential publications.

One of the best known popularized publicists, for example, is Ben Frank of New York. Frank is on very good terms with producers at shows like OPRAH, so he can regularly place his clients on the show. Publicists can be found in the "Public Relations" heading in the Yellow Pages of any large city. The cost for retaining a publicist varies greatly, and can often run into thousands of dollars. And this is without a guarantee of desired results, so your budget may dictate that you select a publicity service that charges by a fee-per-result basis. However, if you want to hire the best, following is a list of America's top publicity services.

Ben Frank Promotion 60 E. 42nd Street New York, NY 10017	KSB Promotions 55 Honey Creek NE Ada, MI 49301
Planned Television Arts 25 W. 43rd Street New York, NY 10036	Associated Release Svc. 2 N. Riverside Plaza Chicago, IL 60606

Essentially, fee-per-service firms have a flat rate for getting an article written about you or your company in a national magazine or getting a book written about you, or placing you on a talk show, etc. Some companies charge a percentage of the cost of the same exposure, if you had had to pay for it through advertisement, but most just say, "If you want this, it's going to cost you that."

Unhumble Enterprises, a unique publicity service, has a fee-per-service price schedule, which at press time was:

Local Newspaper Article	$100
Article in Local Magazine	$150
Article in Regional Magazine	$250
Article in Metro or National Newspaper	$1,000
Article in National Magazine	$1,500
Appearance on Local Radio Show	$100
Appearance on Regional Radio Show	$250
App. on Syndicated/Nat'l Radio Show	$1,000
Appearance on Local TV Show	$400
Appearance on Regional TV Show	$800
Appearance on National TV Show	$5,000
Book Mentioning You or Co. Favorably	$2,000
Book About You or Company	$8,000

At least you know what you're getting, and if they don't or can't deliver, you get your money back. Unhumble Enterprises is a good, reliable firm, and it's run by people who know exactly what the self-promoter is looking for.

> Unhumble Enter.
> 8177 S. Harvard
> Suite 202
> Tulsa, OK 74137

There are several a-la-carte publicity services that offer the same low prices, but are devoted to just one, or perhaps two particular aspects of publicity generation. For example, Professional Broadcasting Services, run by my friend Sherman Harris, specializes in getting your message to hundreds of thousands of radio listeners, by participating in his syndicated national radio talk show. His program airs in many major cities, and for only $600 or so, your message or book or whatever will be heard by millions of listeners.

> Prof. Broadcast Svc.
> Suite 202
> 255 N. El Cielo Road
> Palm Springs, CA
> 92262

If you'd like to be featured in a book, but your budget doesn't allow some of the fees traditionally required, I have a solution for you. Every few months, Phil Dewar Publishing compiles a book using information or statistics supplied by hundreds of ordinary people. If you request it, your name will be included. For example, one of the books they're compiling now is "*Journeys into the Extraordinary: 500 Americans Describe the Strangest, Most Bizarre Event of Their Lives.*" They do not charge for inclusion in the book; in fact, they're very happy to include your information as long as it meets their current needs. For further information, write them for a copy of their participation brochure. Be sure to send an SASE and $1.

> Phil Dewar Publishing
> 3808 Rosecrans Street
> Suite 730
> San Diego, CA 92110

Of course it is entirely possible to achieve all this fame from your own initiative, and save alot of money in the process. If you are serious about this, I highly recommend Dr. Jeffrey Lant's *The Unabashed Self-Promoter's Guide.* It is subtitled "What every man, woman, child and organization in America needs to know about getting ahead by exploiting the media." And that pretty well sums it up. This book, which sells for $39.95, is the bible of getting ahead in life by securing media attention. Although the book has been copied, it has never been equaled in its sheer cleverness. It even shows how to

> JLA Associates
> 50 Follen St #507
> Cambridge, MA
> 02138

get the mayor of your town to proclaim a day in your honor! Dr. Lant practices what he preaches too. No wonder I wanted him to write the foreword to this book!

STATUES AND PLAQUES

One of the better known tricks to immortalize oneself is through art - busts, plaques, statues and the like. And unless you are so brazenly "unabashed" that you can walk right up and commission a plaque about yourself without embarrassment, it would probably be a good idea to have this done through the mail.

> **John Hinds & Co.**
> **81 Greenridge Dr. W.**
> **Elmira, NY 14905**

John Hinds and Company manufactures bronze plaques enscripted with anything the purchaser wants. These are especially nice to place at the base of statues or at the entrance of a historical building. These start at about $60.

Famous Bolivian artist, Rudy Ayoroa will sculpt a bust or full statue based on photographs of you at various angles, and a description of the pose of the statue. Ayoroa's work is in the Hirshorn Museum and Sculpture Garden as well as the National Museum of American Art in Washington, D.C. He publishes no catalog or price list, but write to him with a detailed description of what you want, and he will quote you a price for the work.

> **Rudy Ayoroa**
> **202 Lexington Ave.**
> **Danville, KY 40422**

IMMORTALITY VIA CONTRIBUTIONS

If you have the money, and you seek recognition, there really should be no problem working out a deal with one charity or another. December issues of *Town & Country* sometimes contain a section called "Good Tithings," which offers a pretty impressive list of the honors you can buy, but the entries are pretty pricey. Some examples:

Donation of:	Gets You:
$60,000	a named animal training room - ASPCA
$1 Million	a bust - Cathedral of St. John in NY
$50,000	a diorama - Denver Mus. of Nat. History
$25,000	a named room - Ronald McDonald House
$3.5 Million	a named sculpture garden - National Museum of Women in the Arts
2.5 Million	a named concert hall - Boston Symphony

Not on *Town & Country*'s list but just as interesting is the "Own Your Own Ballet" offer made by Experientia, Ltd. You can take a bow and enjoy a standing ovation for a ballet you helped make possible. You can "own" the ballet performed by the the critically acclaimed Miami City Ballet, and you will be identified as the underwriter in perpetuity each time the ballet is performed by the company. The cost is a whopping $27,500, but it *is* tax-deductible. Write Experientia for further details.

Experientia, Ltd.
419 N. Larchmont
Suite 97
Los Ang., CA 90004

IMMORTALITY UNLIMITED

The "problem" with donating to charity to receive an award or honor is the fact that most of the proceeds go to charitable work, so the price, consequently, is much higher than necessary. Immortality Unlimited does alot of what charities do, but on a for-profit basis. In other words, Immortality Unlimited can very likely arrange the same sort of things listed above, but for about 1/10 or less of the price. They can get buildings and streets named

Immortality Unlimited
3808 Rosecrans Street
Suite 730
San Diego, CA 92110

after you, rivers and creeks named for you, and even a few towns have offered to change their name to Yeagerville or whatever you want, if you'll help relieve their financial problems. What a deal! If you want to truly go down in history, Immortality Unlimited can help you. Send for their catalog which currently costs $4.

YOUR PLACE IN THE COSMOS

Over 300,000 stars have been named for presidents, dignitaries, movie stars, scientists and other VIPs. And now, thanks to the Star Registry, you can join the ranks of those immortal souls who have had stars named after them. International Star Registry is the authority that redesignates star names from the old, boring style like Pegasus RA22H18M355SD1138, to something a little more personal and manageable like Fred Smith 16. The star's new name will be permanently recorded in the next edition of the ISR Directory, and the honoree receives a beautiful certificate as well as two sky charts showing the star's precise location in the sky. Now I'm pretty sure all the good ones like those in the Big Dipper are already spoken for, but you'll still be able to point your little star out to friends. The cost for buying a star is only $40, which is one heck of a deal for those in the market for immortality.

> **International Star Registry**
> **1821 Willow Road**
> **Northfield, IL 60093**

Chapter Nine: More Status For Sale

This final chapter is a catch-all for those status-buying opportunities that really didn't fit anywhere else. And since they are of such a varied nature, they really don't need introducing any better than that.

SEEING AND BEING SEEN

Unhumble Enterprises can not only get you a dinner date with Hollywood stars, royalty and other VIPs, they can also arrange for some of them to spend the weekend in your home! If you'd like to entertain a visiting Prince or movie star, and show them off around town, this is definitely the place. Prices are not all that bad, either. Send $5 for their latest catalog.

> Unhumble Enterprises
> 8177 S. Harvard
> Suite 202
> Tulsa, OK 74137

If having the real thing is a little too costly, you can simply have your picture made with a cardboard cutout of your favorite celebrity. The final photograph of the two of you together looks incredibly lifelike, and you can impress all your friends with your amazing connections. Life-size cutouts are available for everyone from George Bush to Magic Johnson, and they cost about $20 each. Write Advanced Graphics for free details.

> Advanced Graphics
> 982 Howe Road
> Martinez, CA 94553

SPRING TRAINING

Baseball marketing was once one of the great untapped resources in this country. No longer. The New York Mets call it the "Ulti-Met" Week. The Los Angeles Dodgers call it the Ultimate Adult Baseball Camp. All operate in much the same way: exploit the little boy in every red-blooded American male, and offer him a once-in-a-lifetime chance to play with the big-leaguers. These camps last about a week, and contain all the work-outs, batting practice and locker-room chatter of real spring training. All this takes place under the supervision of Major League players. Real live Mets and Dodgers mingle with and compete against these "pay for play" types.

These camps are staffed by the likes of Ernie Banks, Bob Feller, Sandy Koufax, Tom Seaver, Tug McGraw, and oh yes, Tommy Lasorda. In addition to the games, you get the gimmicks - uniforms, baseball cards, videotaped highlights and more. Prices are between $4,000 and $5,000 for the week.

> **Ulti-Met Week**
> **2917 W. Hwy 434**
> **Suite 131**
> **Longwood, FL 32779**
>
> **Dodgertown**
> **P.O. Box 2887**
> **Vero Beach, FL 32961**

Football fans would probably go for camps like these too, but I can understand how insurance companies might cringe at the thought of CPAs and college professors getting mangled by a 300-pound lineman. The Los Angeles Rams have sort of compromised with a program they call "Face The Rams." Rams fans have lunch with the team at the actual training table, and watch practice close-up during a private tour of the Rams camp. The price for this is only $600, and is available from Dreams Come True. If this catches on, I imagine you'll be seeing lots more of this in the near future.

> **Dreams Come True**
> **2753 Glendower Ave**
> **Los Ang. CA 90027**

Other sports fans are not entirely left out of the pay-for-play business. Although ProServ, Inc. is primarily a sports management company, arranging for high-profile sports stars to speak before corporate gatherings and the like, but for the right price, they can set up a singles match with Stephan Edberg or maybe a round of golf with Calvin Peete. Expect the prices to be way up there, but if you've always wanted to go head-to-head with your favorite sports hero, this might be your one chance.

> ProServ, Inc.
> 1101 Wilson Blvd.
> Arlington, VA 22209

INTERNATIONAL CONTACTS

There may be times when you need an overseas friend to purchase or do something for you that you, for one reason or another, cannot. For example, we cannot buy Cuban cigars in the United States, but since there is no such ban in certain other countries, a well-placed friend could probably score a few without any hassles. If you haven't such a contact, here is a list of individuals who represent each continent and whose sole purpose in life is to do your bidding... for a price.

> Wayne Budd, Inc.
> Budd Building
> Eldorado, Ontario
> Canada K0K 1Y0
>
> Victor Leventhal
> GPO 1933
> Sydney, NSW
> Australia 2001
>
> Jaime Guevara
> Casilla 420
> Ambato, Ecudaor
>
> Dr. H. Kaiser
> P.O. Box 71
> Alfred Back Str. 15-12
> A-5027 Salzburg
> Austria
>
> The Manhattan Transfer
> Suite 6, Swee Lin Court
> 36 Soi Lang Suan
> Bangkok 10500
> Thailand

SUPERDAD

It had to happen sooner or later. With the number of single women growing in this country, combined with the already disproportionate number of men versus women, a market was unavoidably created. Since many single women want to experience motherhood, despite the absence of the traditional father/husband, a sperm bank boom is underway, and there is none so prestigious as the Repository for Germinal Choice, or the Nobel Sperm Bank, as it's been labeled by the media.

RGC is the Rolls Royce of sperm banks, and it takes a pretty impressive resume to even be considered for, uh... depositing. They boast of Nobel prize-winning scientists with a history of long-living ancestors. The idea is a little too futuristic for some people to abide, but it fills a real need for alot of people. I'm not sure how the actual deed is done, but you can write them for more details if interested.

```
Rep. for Germinal Choice
450 S. Escondido Blvd.
Escondido, CA 92025
```

BACKSTAGE PASSES

GRF Press has put together a complete guide to obtaining free tickets, backstage passes and special invitations, and it works! Their system for enabling you to reach these lofty heights has been tried and tested over and over again, and they've put the entire procedure in a book, *VIP*. Using this book, anyone should be able to go where they've never gone before and meet all their favorite rock stars, sports heroes, actors and actresses. Their book is $19.95 and is crammed with useful information.

```
GRF Press
2050 Idle Hour Center
Suite 108
Lexington, KY 40502
```

SWISS BANK ACCOUNTS

The idea of a Swiss bank account brings thoughts to mind of international intrigue, hidden millions and secret weekend trips to Zurich. Actually, Swiss banking is very above-board, completely legal for Americans and can be done entirely through the mail. Many Swiss banks will require a rather large initial deposit to open an account, but some cater to the low-end investor. One such bank is Union Bank of Switzerland in Zurich. They have fax machines, everyone speaks English and the initial deposit required to open an account is only $500.

> Union Bank-Switzerland
> 45 Bahnhofstrasse
> 8021 Zurich
> Switzerland

OWN A PIECE OF AMERICA

How would you like to own land in all fifty states? Well now you can thanks to Markline, an interesting gift catalog. It's a real estate deal that doesn't come along very often: a one square inch "farm" in every state in the Union, for only $30. You receive a beautiful deed and a presentation folder with the legal description of all your pieces of property. They'll also frame the deed for a few dollars more. You'll probably want to write for their catalog ($3) before ordering.

> Markline
> P.O. Box 8
> Elmira, NY 14902

ROYAL WARRANTS OF APPOINTMENT

Have you ever wondered what those little coats-of-arms in the corner of some magazine ads are all about? They usually appear in the advertisements of elite foreign companies, like Range Rover or Stolichnaya, and even some high-profile American businesses from time to time.

They are officially called Royal Warrants of Appointment, and are bestowed upon businesses that a reigning monarch patronizes. Once approved, these companies are allowed to use the royal crest in their advertisements, followed by the words, "By Appointment to His Royal Highness, the Prince of Wales" or "By Appointment to the King of Sweden" or whoever decides to issue the appointment. Each royal house is authorized to distribute such honors, but some are stingier than others. The British royal family has collectively issued hundreds of these warrants, while HRIH Prince Alexis d'Anjou, claimant to half the thrones of eastern Europe, has issued only four or five.

When a company receives an appointment, it begins to receive an enormous amount of additional business from status-conscious clientele, and it really is quite a coup for any upscale business to garner this type of endorsement. Antony Boada can arrange royal warrants from various monarchs and sovereign princes around the world. If your business could benefit from royal patronage, write him for more information.

> **Antony Boada**
> c/o Postbus 5065
> 2900 EB Capelle-upon-Yssel
> The Netherlands

BOARDS OF DIRECTORS

There are several charities that are quite happy to have you as an honorary director for the right donation. The honorary board of directors is usually printed right on the charity's stationery along with the "real" directors, and often in such a way that no one can tell the difference. When writing to some of your favorite charities, explain that this is something you'd like to do, and ask what kind of donation would be appropriate. $500 is a good place to start. This sure spruces up a resume, and the best part is it's totally tax-deductible.

"FANTASY ISLAND" BY MAIL

Once In A Lifetime, mentioned throughout this book, is the only company I know of that has a basic philosophy of "Whatever you want, as long as it's legal, let us know, and we'll quote you a price." Not only do they offer the status-enhancing deals mentioned in this book, but will also arrange for some pretty bizarre events: bungee cord jumping in New Zealand, "harem-for-a-day," canoeing down the Amazon, climbing Mount Everest, etc. You'll want to write for their booklet which describes some of their more requested services, and how to apply for a custom-made experience. I'm told they're even planning a trip into outer space by 1999. Their booklet is $5.

> **Once In A Lifetime**
> **9205 SE Clackamas**
> **Suite #419**
> **Clackamas, OR 97015**

THE ULTIMATE NEWSLETTER

If you liked this book, you'll love *The Machiavellian*, a closely-guarded secret among those who subscribe. It doesn't advertise and probably never will, but it is the most clever resource tool for those interested in unusual loopholes and other tricks for getting ahead. Each monthly issue has quite a few *Status For Sale*-like entries, as well as secret information you aren't supposed to know, and dozens of sources for out-of-the-ordinary merchandise. A sample issues is $3, and yearly subscriptions can be had for $25. *The Machiavellian* is highly recommended.

> **The Machiavellian**
> **1209 Casino Ctr. Blvd**
> **Suite 140**
> **Las Vegas, NV 89104**

A FINAL NOTE

As mentioned in the introduction, obsolescence is what makes most access books like this virtually useless after two or three years. Well, not this one. For at least ten years after the publication of Status For Sale (first printing 1992), I am going to be keeping track of the companies listed herein, as well as searching for new and interesting status-buying opportunities that come along. I will make these findings available on a quarterly basis to all Status For Sale readers. For more information write me at the address below.

> **Wayne Yeager**
> **c/o Charter Publications**
> **3119 Isabel Drive**
> **Los Angeles, CA 90065**

For Your Convenience

Some of the books recommended in "Status For Sale" are available from one convenient source, Charter Books. All prices are postpaid and will be shipped immediately. Please send me the following books:

- [ ] *The Passport Report* by W.G. Hill, JD — $120

- [ ] *The Lloyds Report* by W.G. Hill, JD — $120

- [ ] *Independent Guide to Recording* — $20

- [ ] *How To Start Your Own Country* — $15

- [ ] *The Unabashed Self-Promoter's Guide* — $45

- [ ] *1992-1993 Star Guide* — $15

Send a check or money order for the amount at right in US currency made payable to Charter Books.

Total Enclosed _____

Name _____

Address _____

City _____

State or Province _____ Zip _____

**Charter Books
3119 Isabel Drive
Los Angeles, CA 90065**